¡Ánimo – hable español!

D1823008

This edition published 2003 by Caxton Editions an imprint of
The Caxton Publishing Group under Licence from Carrousel MS.
ISBN 184067 4474

©2002 by Carrousel MS. Paris
Photos: Corel Professional Photos, Photo Disc, project photos
Printed in China

A word in advance to the learner

This audio course will help you in various ways to learn Spanish, improve your Spanish or to work on your existing skills more intensively, enabling the learner to master situations in Spanish. This course combines both listening and speaking, and, should you wish, reading and writing. The audio language course can be used in various ways, depending on how much Spanish you can already speak and how you wish to learn.

At the start of each chapter you will hear a jingle which will make you aware of the new chapter. Thus you have the opportunity to prepare yourself for the new chapter and to prepare yourself for the following texts.

You then hear the expressions and sentences which you will often need and which are of importance in the coming chapter. These expressions do not form a dialogue but are there to help you to ease into the chapter. You will need these expressions in Spanish and they are the main expressions used in Spanish.

There then follows a dialogue in each chapter in which you will hear native Spanish speakers in real situations. In this dialogue you will hear the expressions used which you have already heard. Listen to the dialogue as often as you wish to help you improve your vocabulary, speech and pronunciation and repeat the dialogue by returning to the start of the dialogue on the CD and repeat sentence for sentence. Use the pause control on your CD player for this. Following the dialogue there are exercises in each chapter to practise the aspects of Spanish just learned. Each time there is the necessary help to enable you to complete the exercises. There are instructions and examples preceding each exercise so that you hear how the exercise is to be done.

The second part of the course includes the additional grammar explanations which are deliberately separate from the dialogues so that you can concentrate exclusively on the material you are studying. Thus you can either learn to speak and use the language or you can concentrate on improving your basic knowledge of Spanish grammar at another time.

In a further part of the course book you can find information about Spain. These are designed as short lectures and as preparation for a visit to Spain. This information is designed to help you deal with the unique cultural situations, to help you understand other ways of communication and to help you understand Spain and her ways.

In the last part of the course book you can find a vocabulary list. This can help you in various ways: to look up words whilst learning, to improve your skills at the end of the course or also as vocabulary training before you actually begin speaking Spanish and wish to have enough of range of vocabulary to fall back on.

In the course book you will find all the important expressions, dialogues and exercises as well as additional grammar explanations and typically Spanish texts and vocabulary. The course book also contains tips and help for all Spanish learners and the problems often incurred in Spain and in Spanish. You will also come across English translations which are deliberately very close to the Spanish text, and these are there to help you understand the Spanish, even though grammatically they may not be so stylish in English.

The course can of course be used in different ways. The chapters can be used as you please. For example, should you wish to learn Spanish whilst driving in the car, then you only need to listen to the dialogues on the CDs and complete the exercises verbally. You can repeat the dialogue in either verbal or written form, depending on where you are. On the one hand you may just take a look in the book at home when you wish to check up on information, or you may want to complete all the exercises in written form. The same can be done with the vocabulary lists – it all depends on how intensively you want to learn Spanish.

There is no absolutely 'right' system for listening and repeating, reading, listening and speaking or for reading and writing. Complete the course how you wish and repeat as often as necessary. And of course you can take as much time as you wish. At the end of this course you will have recognised the points where English speakers have problems with Spanish in everyday situations. And you will have practised enough to feel more secure when you practise your Spanish in real life situations.

Additional information for those interested in didactics

This course represents the results of the newer findings in foreign language didactics in an audio form. The dialogues which are consistently in authentic Spanish language comprise a rich language surrounding in which one can easily find one's way around in real foreign language situations. Right from the beginning you will learn to 'hear' the most important things for communication. Through the continual repetition of phrases which occur regularly to keep a conversation going you will pick up these phrases.

Contents

Contents

In this lesson you will learn how to:

- greet someone;
- introduce yourself or others;
- enquire about someone's well-being or inform others about your own well-being

 CD1 TOP1 Remember the following expressions and phrases:

Bienvenidos	Welcome
Hola	Hello
Soy Ana.	I am Ana.
Encantado.	Pleased to meet you.
Mi nombre es José Delgado.	My name is José Delgado.
Mucho gusto.	Nice to meet you.
Me llamo Alfonso.	My name is (I am called) Alfonso
Encantada.	Pleased to meet you.
Éste es don José.	This is Don José.
Ésta es doña María.	This is Doña María.
Vivo en Valencia.	I live in Valencia.
Tengo 18 años.	I am 18 years old.
Soy estudiante.	I am a student.
Hola, ¿qué tal?	Hello, how do you do?
Hola, ¿cómo estás?	Hello, how are you?
Estoy bien, gracias.	I am well, thank you.
¿Cómo estás?	How are you?
No estoy mal.	Not bad.
buenos días	good day; good morning
buenas tardes	good day; good evening
buenas noches	good night

CD1 A: DIÁLOGOS
TOP2

The story:
Ana, Alfonso, José and María introduce themselves in turn. They give their names, age and the place where they live. They then introduce the next person.

Ana

Hola, soy Ana. Tengo 18 años. Soy estudiante y vivo en Valencia. Éste es mi amigo Alfonso.	Hello, I am Ana. I am 18 years old and live in Valencia. This is my friend Alfonso.

Alfonso

Yo me llamo Alfonso. Tengo 22 años y soy mecánico. Vivo en Barcelona. Éste es don José.	I am called Alfonso. I am 22 years old and am a mechanic. I live in Barcelona. This is Don José.

José

Mi nombre es José Delgado. Tengo 45 años y soy policía. Vivo en Marbella. Ésta es doña María.	My name is José Delgado. I am 45 years old and am a policeman. I live in Marbella. This is Doña María.

María

Hola, soy María. Tengo 54 años. Soy ama de casa y vivo en Madrid.	Hello, I am Maria. I am 54 years old. I am a housewife and live in Madrid.

The story:
Now a man and a woman introduce themselves to each other.

Man

Hola, soy Ricardo García Ruiz.	Hello, I am Ricardo García Ruiz.

Woman

Encantada. Mi nombre es Eva Martínez Prats.	Pleased to meet you, my name is Eva Martínez Prats.

Man

Mucho gusto.	Delighted to meet you.

Woman

Buenos días, me llamo Rosa Clarín.	Good day. I am called (my name is) Antonio Bueno.

Man

Encantado. Mi nombre es Antonio Bueno.	Pleased to meet you. My name is Antonio Bueno.

9

Woman
Encantada.   Pleased to meet you.

The story:
Ana, Alfonso and José greet each other.

José
Hola, buenos días. ¿Cómo estáis?   Hello, good day. How are you?
Hola, Ana. Hola, Alfonso,   Hello Ana, hello Alfonso.
¿qué tal?   How do you do?

Alfonso
Buenos días, don José, bien, y usted,   Good day Don José, I am
¿cómo está?   well and how are you?

José
No estoy mal.   Not bad.

Ana
Y doña María, ¿cómo está?   And Doña María, how is she?

José
Está muy bien, gracias.   She is very well, thank you.

B: EJERCICIOS

Directions: You will hear various pieces of information which you must use to form complete sentences after hearing the beep. You will then hear the correct answer. You can then compare your response to the correct answer.

You will then be given the opportunity to repeat the correct answer during a further pause.

For each exercise there is an example.

CD1 TOP3 Ejercicio 1:
Forme frases completas – Form complete sentences.

E Ejemplo – Example:

Voice: *Ana; estudiante*

You: *Me llamo Ana. Soy estudiante.*

Voice: *Me llamo Ana. Soy estudiante.*

You: *Me llamo Ana. Soy estudiante.*

11

Y ahora usted, por favor – and now you:

1. *Ana; estudiante*
   Me llamo Ana. Soy estudiante.   I am called Ana. I am a student.

2. *Alfonso; mecánico*
   Me llamo Alfonso. Soy mecánico.   I am called Alfonso.
   I am a mechanic.

3. *José; policía*
   Me llamo José. Soy policía.   I am called José. I am a policeman.

4. *María; ama de casa*
   Me llamo María. Soy ama de casa.   I am called María. I am a housewife.

5. *Lola; secretaria*
   Me llamo Lola. Soy secretaria.   I am called Lola. I am a secretary.

6. *Julia; profesora*
   Me llamo Julia. Soy profesora.   I am called Julia. I am a teacher.

7. *Toni; arquitecto*
   Me llamo Toni. Soy arquitecto.   I am called Toni. I am an architect.

CD1 TOP4 Ejercicio 2:

Repita – Listen to the numbers and repeat them:

1	uno	11	once
2	dos	12	doce
3	tres	13	trece
4	cuatro	14	catorce
5	cinco	15	quince
6	seis	16	dieciséis
7	siete	17	diecisiete
8	ocho	18	dieciocho
9	nueve	19	diecinueve
10	diez	20	veinte

21	veintiuno	40	cuarenta
22	veintidós	50	cincuenta
23	veintitrés	60	sesenta
24	veinticuatro	70	setenta
25	veinticinco	80	ochenta
26	veintiséis	90	noventa
27	veintisiete	100	cien
28	veintiocho		
29	veintinueve		
30	treinta		
31	treinta y uno		
32	treinta y dos		
33	treinta y tres		
34	treinta y cuatro		
...			

Indique su edad en una frase completa – Give your age using a complete sentence.

E **Ejemplo – Example:**

Voz:	*Dieciocho*
Usted:	*Tengo dieciocho años.*
Voz:	*Tengo dieciocho años.*
Usted:	*Tengo dieciocho años.*

 Y ahora usted, por favor – and now you:

1. Dieciocho
   Tengo dieciocho años.   I am 18 years old.

2. Veintidós
   Tengo veintidós años.   I am 22 years old.

3. Cuarenta y cinco
   Tengo cuarenta y cinco años.   I am 45 years old.

4. Cincuenta y cuatro
   Tengo cincuenta y cuatro años.   I am 54 years old.

5. Dieciséis
   Tengo dieciséis años.   I am 16 years old.

6. treinta y tres
   Tengo treinta y tres años.   I am 33 years old.

7. sesenta y dos
   Tengo sesenta y dos años.   I am 62 years old.

Ejercicio 3:

Forme frases completas – say where the person mentioned lives using a complete sentence. In doing so, leave out the personal pronoun.

E Ejemplo – Example:

Voz:	*yo; Valencia*
Usted:	*Vivo en Valencia.*
Voz:	*Vivo en Valencia.*
Usted:	*Vivo en Valencia.*

 Y ahora usted, por favor – and now you:

1. yo; Valencia
   Vivo en Valencia.   I live in Valencia.

2. ella; Alicante
   Vive en Alicante.   She lives in Alicante.

3. tú; Bilbao
   Vives en Bilbao.   You live in Bilbao.

4. ellos; Cádiz
   Viven en Cádiz.   They live in Cádiz.

5. Nosotros; Granada
   Vivimos en Granada.   We live in Granada.

6. él; Burgos
   Vive en Burgos.   He lives in Burgos.

7. Vosotros; Madrid
   Vivís en Madrid.   You live in Madrid.

GRAMÁTICA

The Salutation – el saludo

The informal Spanish form of greeting *hola* is roughly equivalent to the English "Hello",
but is even more widespread and is often combined with other forms. For
example *,hola, ¿qué tal?, hola, ¿cómo estás?* "Hello, how do you do?". *Hola* can
be used at any time of the day.
The following are more formal forms of greeting and are restricted to a particular
time of day.

In the morning before noon:	*buenos días* (literal translation: good day)
From noon until dinner:	*buenas tardes* (literal translation: good afternoon)
In the evening:	*buenas noches* (literal translation: good night)

Buenas noches is also used before going to bed: *buenas noches* – good night.

¿qué tal? is a set phrase for asking how someone is. It does not change its form. It
is the equivalent of "how do you do?". However *¿qué tal?* is a polite form rather
than a real question. The person you are talking to does not expect you to go into
detail about your well-being.

Examples:
> *Hola, Alfonso, ¿qué tal?*
> *Hola, don José, ¿qué tal?*
> *Hola, Ana y doña María, ¿qué tal?*

Another way of inquiring about a person's well-being is to use the question
¿cómo estás? In this case though, it is not an invariant set phrase. Like other
languages (other than English) the verb ending changes depending on the
people involved in the exchange. A distinction between singular and plural
must be made as well as a distinction between the familiar form of you *tú* and
the polite form of you *usted*.

Examples:
José:	*Hola, Alfonso, ¿cómo estás?*
José:	*Hola, Alfonso, hola, Ana, ¿cómo estáis?*

José:	Hola Alfonso, ¿cómo estás?
Alfonso:	Hola, don José, ¿cómo está usted?

Alfonso:	Hola, doña María, ¿cómo está usted?
Alfonso:	Hola, doña María, hola, don José, ¿cómo están ustedes?

How to Introduce Yourself and Others

To introduce yourself you can use either *soy* (I am) or *me llamo* (literal translation: I call myself) or *mi nombre* es (my name is – this form is relatively formal and is mostly used when the surname is also mentioned).

Examples:

Ana:	Soy Ana.
Alfonso:	Me llamo Alfonso.
José:	Mi nombre es José Delgado.
María:	Soy María.

Other than in very formal situations it is not usual in Spain to use your surname during an introduction. Normally you introduce yourself with your first name and only use this amongst friends, people of the same age and social standing. Otherwise you can add the polite forms *don* (for men) and *doña* (for women). You have probably heard of the famous Don Juan.

 Let's once again hear how our main characters introduce themselves to each other.

Ana:	Éste es Alfonso.
Alfonso:	Éste es don José.
José:	Ésta es doña María.

Caution: The fact that people are on first-name terms does not by any means imply that they use the informal grammatical forms when talking to each other!

When two people introduce themselves to each other it is usual to use the polite forms *encantado, -a* (lit. enchanted) or *mucho gusto* (lit. I like a lot):

Examples:

señor:	Soy Ricardo García Ruiz.
señora:	Encantada. Mi nombre es Eva Martínez Prats.
señor:	Mucho gusto.

The Verb *estar* – el verbo *estar*

The verb *estar* is irregular and is conjugated as follows in the present tense:

		ESTAR (Present)
Singular	1. Pers.	*(yo) estoy*
	2. Pers.	*(tú) estás*
	3. Pers.	*(él/ella/usted) está*
Pluria	1. Pers.	*(nosotros/nosotras) estamos*
	2. Pers.	*(vosotros/vosotras) estáis*
	3. Pers.	*(ellos/ellas/ustedes) están*

When asked about his well-being our friend replied:

Alfonso:	*Estamos bien.*
José:	*No estoy mal.*
José:	*María está muy bien.*

Estoy bien	(literally: I am good)
Estoy muy bien.	I am very well.
Estoy mal	I am not (feeling) well.
Estoy muy mal.	I am not (feeling) at all well.
No estoy mal.	OK (literally: I am not bad).

Use of the Personal Pronoun

You will already have noticed that an equivalent for the personal pronoun *I* was not used in the Spanish sentences. This doesn't mean though that Spanish does not have a word corresponding to *I*. Personal pronouns, however, are used far more seldomly in Spanish than in English – specifically, when the person speaking wants to emphasise that those mentioned rather than others are the subject of what is being discussed. Examples: **Alfonso es mecánico y yo soy estudiante. María es ama de casa y yo soy policía.**

For this reason we will only give the personal pronouns in the first example of a verb conjugation.

The Cardinal Numbers

1	uno
2	dos
3	tres
4	cuatro
5	cinco
6	seis
7	siete
8	ocho
9	nueve
10	diez

11	once
12	doce
13	trece
14	catorce
15	quince

Above 16 counting gets easier. The numbers then repeat themselves in various combinations:

16	dieciséis
17	diecisiete
18	dieciocho
19	diecinueve
20	veinte

For numbers starting with 20 the final -e of *veinte* is omitted:

21	veintiuno
22	veintidós
23	veintitrés
24	veinticuatro
25	veinticinco
26	veintiséis
27	veintisiete
28	veintiocho
29	veintinueve

Above 30 counting is regular and combined numbers are not compounded:

30	treinta
31	treinta y uno
32	treinta y dos
33	treinta y tres
34	treinta y cuatro

and so on. The remaining multiples of ten are:

40	cuarenta
50	cincuenta
60	sesenta
70	setenta
80	ochenta
90	noventa
100	cien

Conjugation of Regular Verbs Ending in -*ir*

The verb *vivir* is conjugated regularly. It belongs to the conjugation of verbs ending in -*ir*. In all there are three classes of verb (conjugations of verb):
Verbs ending in -*ar* such as **tomar**
Verbs ending in -*er* such as **comer**
Verbs ending in -*ir* such as **vivir**

		VIVIR (Present)
	1. Pers.	*vivo*
Singular	2. Pers.	*vives*
	3. Pers.	*vive*
	1. Pers.	*vivimos*
Plural	2. Pers.	*vivís*
	3. Pers.	*viven*

Example
Ana: – *Vivo en Valencia.* – I live in Valencia.
Spanish uses the same word *vivir* as in English to mean to live, in the sense of to be alive (to exist) and to inhabit.

The Demonstrative Pronoun

You have probably noticed that two different forms were used for the demonstrative pronoun, *éste* and *ésta*:

Example
    Alfonso: – *Éste es don José.*
    José: – *Ésta es doña María.*

Éste replaces a masculine noun and *ésta* replaces a feminine noun.

Punctuation

In a Spanish question, the question mark does not only appear at the end of the sentence, but also inverted at the beginning. The same thing applies to the exclamation mark.

Rules for commas are not the same as for English. There is usually a comma where a pause would occur when speaking.

Information about the Country

The greeting

Except in very formal situations, it is normal in Spain for women to greet each other, first by kissing the left then the right cheek. It is mostly a matter of the meaning conveyed by the kisses. Men and women also greet each other with kisses, but not with the same regularity. Men greet each other with a handshake, and when they know each other well and haven't seen each other for a while, they also tap each other lightly on the shoulders.

LECCIÓN 2
En la cafetería

In this lesson you will learn how to:

- make an order in a café
- tell the time
- say goodbye

CD1
TOP6 Remember the following expressions and phrases:

¿Qué tomáis?	What are you going to have? (2 pers. plural form)
un té con limón	a lemon tea
un bocadillo de queso	a cheese roll
una taza de chocolate	a cup of (hot) chocolate
un café con leche	a white coffee
un café solo	a black coffee
una tostada con mantequilla	(some) toast with butter
una tostada con aceite y tomate	(some) toast with (oil) olive oil and tomato
muy bien	very well; yes
Son las diez.	It is ten o'clock.
adiós	Goodbye
hasta luego	Bye; till later
hasta pronto	see you soon (lit: until soon)
Me alegro mucho de veros.	Nice to see you.

A: DIÁLOGOS

CD1 **The story:**
TOP7
Ana, Alfonso und Don José place their order in the café.

Waitress
Buenos días.   Good Day.

José
Buenos días.   Good Day.

Waitress
¿Qué toman los señores?   What would you like?

José
¿Qué tomáis vosotros dos?   What are you two going to have?

Ana
Yo un té con limón y un bocadillo   I (am going to have) a lemon tea
de queso   and a cheese roll.

Alfonso
Yo una taza de chocolate y   I (am going to have) a hot chocolate
una tostada.   and some toast.

José
Yo también una tostada, pero con   I am also going to have some toast
un café con leche.   but with a white coffee.

Waitress
Muy bien, un té con limón, un   So that's a lemon tea,
bocadillo de queso, una taza de   a cheese roll, a cup of hot chocolate,
chocolate, dos tostadas y un café   two (portions) of toast and a
con leche. Las tostadas, ¿con   white coffee; the toast with butter
mantequilla o con aceite?   or oil (olive oil)?

Alfonso
Yo con matequilla, por favor.   For me with butter please.

José
Y yo con tomate y aceite.   And for me with tomato and oil.

Waitress
Muy bien. Gracias.   OK. Thank you.

25

The story:

After having breakfast together it is time to say goodbye:

José

Bueno, amigos, ya son las diez y media. Hora de irse. Me alegré mucho de veros.	Now friends, it is already half past ten. Time to go. It was nice to see you.

Ana

Adiós, Don José, hasta luego, Alfonso.	Goodbye, Don José, bye (till later), Alfonso.

Alfonso

Adiós y hasta pronto.	Goodbye and see you soon.

Waitress

Hasta pronto, señores.	See you soon gentlemen (and ladies).

 **B: EJERCICIOS**

Ejercicio 1:
Forme frases completas – Form complete sentences using the appropriate form of the verb "tomar".

 Ejemplo – Example:

Voz: *Juan; un café con leche*

Usted: *Juan toma un café con leche.*

Voz: *Juan toma un café con leche.*

Usted: *Juan toma un café con leche.*

1.
2.
3.

 Y ahora usted, por favor – and now you:

1. Juan; un café con leche
   Juan toma un café con leche.   Juan has a white coffee.

2. yo; una tostada con mantequilla
   Tomo una tostada con mantequilla.   I have (some) toast with butter.

3. Ellos; té con limón
   Toman té con limón.   They have some lemon tea.

4. Nosotros; café solo
   Tomamos café solo.   We drink black coffee.

5. tú; una tostada con tomate y aceite
   Tomas una tostada con tomate   You have toast with tomato and oil.
   y aceite.

6. María; una taza de chocolate
   Toma una taza de chocolate.   María has a cup of hot chocolate.

7. Vosotros; un bocadillo de queso
   Tomáis un bocadillo de queso.   You have a cheese roll.

 Ejercicio 2:

Indique la hora – Give the time. We will start with "Son las diez"
Add a quarter of an hour in each case.

 Ejemplo – Example:

Voz:	*Son las diez.*
Usted:	*Son las diez y cuarto.*
Voz:	*Son las diez y cuarto.*
Usted:	*Son las diez y cuarto.*

Y ahora usted, por favor – and now you:

1. Son las diez.   It is ten o'clock.
   Son las diez y cuarto.   It is a quarter past ten.

2. Son las diez y cuarto.   It is a quarter past ten.
   Son las diez y media.   It is half past ten.

3. Son las nueve menos cuarto.   It is a quarter to nine.
   Son las nueve.   It is nine o'clock.

4. Son las nueve y media.   It is half past nine.
   Son las diez menos cuarto.   It is a quarter to ten.

5. Son las ocho.   It is eight o'clock.
   Son las ocho y cuarto.   It is a quarter past eight.

6. Son las cuatro y media.   It is half past four.
   Son las cinco menos cuarto.   It is a quarter to five.

7. Son las tres y cuarto.   It is a quarter past three.
   Son las tres y media.   It is half past three.

Ejercicio 3 (ejercicio fonético):
Repita – Repeat:

E **Ejemplo – Example:**

Voz:	*me alegro*
Usted:	*me alegro*
Voz:	*me alegro*
Usted:	*me alegro*

 Y ahora usted, por favor – and now you:

me alegro ...
ésta es doña Ana ...
éste es don Antonio ...
mi amigo ...
don Alfonso ...
son las ocho ...

tengo ...
té ...
tomamos ...
taza ...
tomate ...
treinta y tres ...

don José ...
doña María ...
dos cafés ...

buenos días ...
diez ...
dieciocho ...

policía ...
profesora ...
por favor ...
ama de casa ...
¿qué tal?
¿cómo estás? ...

ustedes ...
media ...
Madrid ...
Málaga ...
hasta luego ...
amigo ...
Cuba ...
Bilbao ...
San Sebastián ...

Barcelona ...
diez ...
dieciocho ...
cinco ...
aceite ...
Zaragoza ...

Rafael ...
Rita ...
Rosa ...
Ramón ...
Rodrigo ...
Roma ...

María ...
Granada ...
hora ...

nombre ...
Bárbara ...
treinta y tres ...

bocadillo ...
mantequilla ...
me llamo Alfonso ...
Marbella ...
ella ...
ellos ...

hola ...
hora de irse ...
hasta luego ...
hasta pronto ...
hasta la vista ...
hasta la próxima ...

Sevilla ...
Salamanca ...
San Sebastián ...
secretaria ...
señor ...
señora ...

Valencia ...
hasta la vista ...
vivo en Valencia ...
vive en Valladolid ...
vivimos en Vigo ...
vosotros ...

GRAMÁTICA

The Verb *"tomar"* – el verbo *"tomar"*

Tomar algo basically means *to consume something* or *to have something.* It can be used to mean "to drink" as well as "to eat".

Example:

Tomo una tostada.	I eat toast.
Tomo un café.	I drink coffee.

The verb ***tomar*** is conjugated regularly.

CONJUGATION OF REGULAR VERBS ENDING IN *-AR*

TOMAR (Present)

Singular	1. Pers.	*tomo*
	2. Pers.	*tomas*
	3. Pers.	*toma*
Plural	1. Pers.	*tomamos*
	2. Pers.	*tomáis*
	3. Pers.	*toman*

All regular verbs whose infinitive ends in *-ar* are conjugated using this pattern.

 **Caution:** In Spanish spoken in Latin-America *tomar* means to drink alcohol, for example, *Ricardo toma mucho.* – Ricardo drinks a lot.

The Time

To tell the time you use the following construction

son + *las* + **Time**

Examples: *Son las diez.*
                 Son las dos.

                 Es la una.

The half hours are added to the full hours:

Examples:

It is half past nine.   *Son las nueve y media.*
(literally "it is nine and half")
It is half past ten.   *Son las diez y media.*

The quarter hours are formed in the same way as in English.

the quarter *el cuarto*
Examples:
It is a quarter past ten.   *Son las diez y cuarto.*
(literally: it is ten and quarter.)
It is a quarter to ten.   *Son las diez menos cuarto.*
(literally: it is ten minus quarter.)

To ask the time you say *¿qué hora es?* When replying you don't need to repeat the verb:

¿Qué hora es?
Las nueve y diez.

¿Qué hora es?
La una menos cinco.

The word *hora* has different meanings depending on the context:

hora de irse   **Time** to go
¿Qué hora es?   What **time** ist es?
una hora   an **hour**

Muy vs. mucho

Muy and *mucho* are adverbs which can be translated with *very*. They differ in the way they are used. The adverb *mucho* comes after the verb:

Example:
    Me alegro mucho.   I am very pleased.

The adverb *muy* comes before the adjective or another adverb:

Example:
    Estoy muy bien.   I am very well.

Information about the Country

When you order a coffee you must also say whether you would like it with or without milk:

    un café con leche   a white coffee (coffee with milk)
    un café solo   a black coffee

If you want milk this often comes in relatively large quantities already poured into the coffee.

Rolls or toast are served in Spain with either butter or olive oil. A Catalan variant, which is also a favourite all over Spain, is toast served with tomato and olive oil. The tomato is spread on the bread. Pepper and salt is then added and finally olive oil is dribbled over the tomato.

Examples:

una tostada con mantequilla	toast with butter
una tostada con aceite	toast with oil
una tostada con aceite y tomate	toast with oil and tomato

And now we come to forms used to say goodbye:

For foreigners the form _hasta la vista_ is probably the best-known way of saying goodbye in Spanish. However you will not hear this form in Spain as often as you might think.
The expression **adiós** is far more commen. You should also note that the Spanish also use **adiós** to greet each other when passing each in the street. In this case **adiós** really means **good morning** or **good day.**

Example:
  Good day (hello), Don José.   _Adiós, don José._

A more casual way of saying goodbye is to use the expression **hasta luego**. Literally translated this means "until later". However "later" does not necessarily refer to the same day.

The phrase **hasta pronto**, literally translated as "till soon", is used by the person speaking to indirectly suggest that he won't be seeing the person he is talking to for a longer period of time and that he hopes to see him again soon.

Hasta la próxima (literally translated: until the next (time)) is a far more common way of saying goodbye.

A polite form frequently used after a brief encounter is
me alegro mucho de veros, which roughly means "it was nice to meet you" (literally translated: I am glad to see you).

Some comments on pronunciation

Vowels

In Spanisch there are only 5 vowels:
a, e, i, o and u

In Spanish the vowels are pronounced smoothly, for example "me alegro": both words are not separated clearly like "me / alegro" but more like "mælegro".

Consonants

Many of the Spanish consonants differ from English consonants, so we will explain the most important differences, in order to avoid mistakes in pronunciation:

Sounds like /t/ and /d/ are produced by moving the tongue towards the teeth:

Example: té [té] and not [tʰé]
director [director] and not [diRectʰoR]

/p/ and /k/ are not voiced

Example:

[poliθía] (policía), not [pʰoliθía]
[kása] (casa), not [khása]

Voiced sounds like /b/, /d/ und /g/ are fricatives, when appearing in the middle of a word. This is rather unusal in English and should be practised thoroughly:

Example:

[tostáda] (tostada), not [tʰostʰáda]
[amígo] (amigo), not [amígʰo]
[kúba] (Cuba), not [kʰúba]

The Spanish sound /θ/ is very similar to the English th, although pronounced more emphatically:

Example:

[poliθía] (policía) and not [pʰolisía].

The famous Spanish /r/ is probably the most difficult letter to pronounce. Let the tip of the tongue touch the socket of the teeth, and let a powerful stream of air escape through the mouth, producing a nearly unnoticable vibration in the tip of the tongue.
Use the words "perro" (dog) and „pero" (but) to practise this difference in pronunciation. The /e/ in "perro" is short, the /rr/ is pronounced as described, whilst the e in "pero" is long.

Try to replace the simple /r/ of "María", "Granada" or "Barbara" with a /d/ (Madía, Gdanada, Bádbada) and you will be surprised, how near it comes to the proper way of pronunciation.

A letter not known in English is the "ll", as in "bocadillo" (sandwich). It is treated as a separate letter in the Spanish alphabet: ... jota, ka, ele, elle, eme, ene ... .

Depending on where in Spain or in South-America you are, there are three different ways of pronouncing the "ll":

In several regions of Spain (Andalucia, Extremadura, Murcia and Canary Islands) the "ll" is similar to the English "y", like "young" ("bocadiyo"). This is probably the easiest way for you.

In other parts of Spain we have a slight modification. You can hear an ordinary "l" preceding the actual sound "y", like in "Mallorca" (Malyorca)

In most parts of South-America the „ll" is pronounced as /g/ (fricative), as we know it in the English "gentle", "jam" or "generous".

The Spanish consonant /h/ is mute, although it exists in words like

"hotel" (pronounced "otél").

LECCIÓN 3

Un fin de semana en Granada

In this lesson you will learn how to:

- describe a hotel room
- ask how much something costs
- say how much something costs
- spell out something
- make a suggestion

CD1
TOP 11 Remember the following expressions and phrases:

un hotel de cuatro estrellas	a four-star hotel
un hotel en el centro	a hotel in the town centre
una habitación doble	a double room
una habitación individual	a single room
una habitación con baño o ducha	a room with bath or shower
¿Cuánto cuesta?	How much does it cost?
El desayuno está incluído en el precio.	Breakfast is included in the price.
Está muy bien.	(That is) very good.
Vamos a reservar dos habitaciones	Let's reserve two rooms
por dos noches.	for two nights.
entre los dos	both together (between the two)
Mi nombre es Alfonso García.	My name is Alfonso García.
Tenemos reservadas dos habitaciones.	We have reserved two rooms.
un momento, por favor	one moment please
¿Cómo se escribe?	How do you write (spell) that?

el alfabeto español:

a	ene
be	eñe
ce	o
che	pe
de	cu
e	erre
efe	ese
ge	te
hache	u
i	uve
jota	uve doble
ka	equis
ele	i griega
elle	zeta
eme	

A: DIÁLOGOS

The story:

Alfonso wants to go with his friend Francisco to Granada for the weekend. Before they can start their trip they must reserve a hotel room in Granada. For this purpose they have obtained a hotel guide and are now studying it together.

Alfonso
Aquí tengo una guía de hoteles de Granada. Hay pensiones, hostales y hoteles de hasta cinco estrellas.

I have a hotel guide for Granada here. There are guest houses, hostels and hotels with up to five stars.

Francisco
Yo quiero un hotel de cuatro estrellas en el centro.

I would like a four-star hotel in the city centre.

Alfonso
Un hotel céntrico de cuatro estrellas, ... bien. Aquí tengo un mapa de Granada. En el centro hay 13 hoteles de cuatro estrellas.

A four-star hotel in the city centre ... OK. I have a street-map of Granada here. In the city centre there are 13 four-star hotels.

Francisco

¿Cuánto cuestan?	How much do they cost?

Alfonso

Mira, por ejemplo el Hotel Meliá: es uno de los hoteles más céntricos. La habitación doble cuesta 17.500 pesetas y la habitación individual cuesta 14.000 pesetas. Todas las habitaciones tienen baño o ducha, calefacción central, aire acondicionado, teléfono, televisión, caja fuerte y minibar, y el desayuno está incluído en el precio.

Look, the Hotel Meliá for example: it is one of the most central hotels. A double room costs 17,500 pesetas and a single room costs 14,000 pesetas. All rooms have a bath or shower, central heating, air-conditioning, telephone, TV, a safe and a mini-bar, and breakfast is included in the price.

Francisco

Está muy bien. Vamos a reservar dos habitaciones individuales para dos noches.

That's very good. Let's reserve two single rooms for two nights.

The story:
Alfonso and Francisco have in the meantime arrived at the Hotel Meliá in Granada. At the reception:

Receptionnist

Buenas tardes, señores.

Good evening, gentlemen.

Alfonso

Buenas tardes, mi nombre es Alfonso García y éste es Don Francisco Sánchez. Tenemos reservadas dos habitaciones individuales para dos noches.

Good evening, my name is Alfonso García, and this Mr. Francisco Sánchez. We have reserved two single rooms for two nights.

Receptionnist

Un momento, por favor. El señor Alfonso García Jiménez y el señor Francisco Sánchez Medina, dos habitaciones individuales para los días veintitrés y veinticuatro de mayo, correcto. Jiménez, ¿cómo se escribe, con ge o con jota?

One moment please. Mr. Alfonso García Jiménez and Mr. Francisco Sánchez Medina, two single rooms for the 23rd and 24th May. How do you spell Jiménez, with a "g" or a "j"?

Alfonso
Con jota.   With a "j".

Receptionnist
Y Medina, ¿con ele o con de?   And Medina, with an "l" or a "d"?

Francisco
Con de, con de.   With a "d".

Receptionnist
Muy bien.   Good.

B: EJERCICIOS

CD1 Ejercicio 1:
TOP 13
Calcule – Calculate.

E Ejemplo – Example:

Voz: *Francisco tiene dos euros y Alfonso tiene tres euros.*
             ¿Cuánto dinero tienen entre los dos?
             Francisco has two euros and Alfonso has three euros.
             How much money do they have between them?

Usted: *Entre los dos tienen cinco euros.*
             Between them they have five euros.

Voz: *Entre los dos tienen cinco euros.*

Usted: *Entre los dos tienen cinco euros.*

Y ahora usted, por favor – and now you:

1. Francisco tiene dos euros y
   Alfonso tiene tres euros. ¿Cuánto
   dinero tienen entre los dos?
   Entre los dos tienen cinco euros.

   Francisco has two pounds and Alfonso
   has three euros. How much
   money do they have between them?
   Between them they have five euros.

2. Ana tiene doscientos euros y
   María tiene cien euros.
   ¿Cuánto dinero tienen entre
   las dos?
   Entre las dos tienen trescientos
   euros.

   Ana has 200 euros and María
   has 100 euros.
   How much money do they
   have between them?
   Between them they have 300 euros.

3. Eva tiene trescientas cincuenta
   pesetas y Rosa tiene mil pesetas.
   ¿Cuánto dinero tienen entre las dos?
   Entre las dos tienen mil trescientas
   cincuenta pesetas.

   Eva has 350 pesetas and Rosa
   has 1000 pesetas. How much
   money do they have between them?
   Between them they have
   1,350 pesetas.

4. Carlos tiene cinco mil quinientas
   pesetas y Julia tiene cinco mil
   trescientas pesetas. ¿Cuánto dinero
   tienen entre los dos?
   Entre los dos tienen diez mil
   ochocientas pesetas.

   Carlos has 5,500 pesetas an
   Julia has 5,300 pesetas.
   How much money do they
   have between them?
   Between them they have
   10800 pesetas.

5. Lola tiene quince mil ochocientos
   euros y Pilar tiene mil euros.
   ¿Cuánto dinero tienen entre las dos?
   Entre las dos tienen dieciséis mil
   ochocientos euros.

   Lola has 15,800 euros and
   Pilar has 1,000 euros. How much
   money do they have between them?
   Between them they have
   16,800 euros.

6. Antonio tiene quince euros y
   Ramón tiene quinientos euros.
   ¿Cuánto dinero tienen entre los dos?
   Entre los dos tienen quinientos
   quince euros.

   Antonio has 15 euros and
   Ramón has 500 euros. How much
   money do they have between them?
   Between them they have
   515 euros.

7. Miguel tiene catorce mil euros y
Menchu tiene diez mil euros.
¿Cuánto dinero tienen entre los dos?
Entre los dos tienen veinticuatro mil
euros.

Miguel has 14,000 euros and
Menchu has 10,000 euros. How much
money do they have between them?
Between them they have
24,000 euros.

Ejercicio 2:

Diga que sí – Answer the following questions in the affirmative.

E **Ejemplo – Example:**

Voz: *¿Vais a desayunar en una cafetería?*
Are you going to have breakfast in a café?

Usted: *Sí, vamos a desayunar en una cafetería.*
Yes, we are going to have breakfast in a café.

Voz: *Sí, vamos a desayunar en una cafetería.*

Usted: *Sí, vamos a desayunar en una cafetería.*

Y ahora usted, por favor – and now you:

1. ¿Vais a desayunar en una cafetería?
   Sí, vamos a desayunar en una .
   cafetería

   Are you going to have breakfast
   in a café? Yes, we are going to have
   breakfast in a café.

2. ¿Vais a cenar en un restaurante?
   Sí, vamos a cenar en un restaurante.

   Are you going to have dinner in a
   restaurant? Yes, we are going to have
   dinner in a restaurant.

3. ¿Vais a reservar una habitación
   doble en un hotel céntrico?
   Si, vamos a reservar una habitación
   doble en un hotel céntrico.

   Are you going to reserve a double
   room in a centrally-located hotel?
   Yes, we are going to reserve a double
   room in a centrally-located hotel.

4. ¿Vais a bailar a una discoteca?

   Si, vamos a bailar a una discoteca.

   Are you going to dance in a
   discotheque?
   Yes, we are you going to dance in a
   discotheque.

5. ¿Vais a tomar un café con leche y
   una tostada con mantequilla?
   Si, vamos a tomar un café con leche
   y una tostada con mantequilla.

   Are you going to have white coffee
   and toast with butter?
   Yes we are going to have white coffee
   and toast with butter.

6. ¿Vais a ir a Granada a un hotel de
   cuatro estrellas?
   Si, vamos a ir a Granada a un hotel
   de cuatro estrellas.

   Are you going to go to a
   four-star hotel in Granada?
   Yes, we you going to go to a
   four-star hotel in Granada.

7. ¿Vais a comer en el hotel?
   Sí, vamos a comer en el hotel.

   Are you going to eat in the hotel?
   Yes, we are going to eat in the hotel.

CD1 TOP15 Ejercicio 3:

Responda usted, por favor – reply to the question.

E Ejemplo – Example:

Voz: *Jiménez, ¿cómo se escribe?*
Jiménez, how do you spell that?

Usted: *Jiménez se escribe jota, i,*
eme, e, ene, e, zeta

Voz: *Jiménez se escribe jota, i,*
eme, e, ene, e, zeta

Usted: *Jiménez se escribe jota, i,*
eme, e, ene, e, zeta

 Y ahora usted, por favor – and now you:

1. Jiménez, ¿cómo se escribe?   Jiménez, how do you spell that?
   Jiménez se escribe jota, i, eme, e,
   ene, e, zeta

2. Medina, ¿cómo se escribe?   Medina, how do you spell that?
   Medina se escribe eme, e, de,
   i, ene, a

3. Carmen, ¿cómo se escribe?   Carmen, how do you spell that?
   Carmen se escribe ce, a, erre,
   eme, e, ene

4. Juan, ¿cómo se escribe?
Juan se escribe jota, u, a, ene

Juan, how do you spell that?

5. Barcelona, ¿cómo se escribe?
Barcelona se escribe be, a, erre, ce, e, ele, o, ene, a

Barcelona, how do you spell that?

6. Valencia, ¿cómo se escribe?
Valencia se escribe uve, a, ele, e, ene, ce, i, a

Valencia, how do you spell that?

7. España, ¿cómo se escribe?
España se escribe e, ese, pe, a, eñe, a

Spain, how do you spell that?

GRAMÁTICA

The Verb *"tener"* – el verbo *"tener"*

The verb *tener* (to have) is conjugated irregularly.

		TENER (Present)
Singular	1. Pers. 2. Pers. 3. Pers.	*tengo* *tienes* *tiene*
Plural	1. Pers. 2. Pers. 3. Pers.	*tenemos* *tenéis* *tienen*

Examples:

*Aquí **tengo** una guía de hoteles.*	Here I have a hotel guide.
*Todas las habitaciones **tienen** baño.*	All rooms have a bath.

El guía

The word *guía* can refer to a person as well as to an information brochure. When *guía* is used to refer to a brochure, it is always in the feminine form *la* guía, e.g.:

la guía de hoteles	the hotel guide
la guía gastronómica	the restaurant guide
la guía telefónica	the telephone directory or telephone list

If *guía* refers to a person then a distinction must be made between *el guía* (the [male] guide) and *la* guía (the[female] guide):

Examples:

el guía de turismo	*la guía de turismo*
(the [male] tourist guide)	(the [female] tourist guide)
el guía del museo	*a guía del museo*
(the [male] museum guide)	(the [female] museum guide)

The Numbers from 100 to 1000

100	cien	600	seiscientos
200	doscientos	700	setecientos
300	trescientos	800	ochocientos
400	cuatrocientos	900	novecientos
500	quinientos	1000	mil

Most multiples of a hundred are formed regularly with the exception of *quinientos, setecientos* and *novecientos*.
Hundreds between 200 and 900 change their ending depending on the gender of the noun they refer to. Hundreds end in *–os* if the following noun is masculine and in *-as* if it is feminine.

Examples:

el franco	⇒	doscientos francos
la peseta	⇒	doscientas pesetas
el euro	⇒	doscientos euros

Tengo trescientos cincuenta francos.
Juan tiene quinientas treinta pesetas.
Cati tiene seiscientos euros.

A propos: Five pesetas are *one duro*,
100 pesetas *veinte duros*.

The thousands are regular.

1000	mil	6000	seis mil
2000	dos mil	7000	siete mil
3000	tres mil	8000	ocho mil
4000	cuatro mil	9000	nueve mil
5000	cinco mil	10 000	diez mil

and so on.

The Verb *"querer"* – el verbo *"querer"*

The verb **querer** (to want, to like) is conjugated irregularly.

		QUERER (Present)
	1. Pers.	*quiero*
Singular	2. Pers.	*quieres*
	3. Pers.	*quiere*
	1. Pers.	*queremos*
Plural	2. Pers.	*queréis*
	3. Pers.	*quieren*

Examples:

Francisco quiere un hotel de cuatro estrellas en el centro.	Francisco wants a four-star hotel in the city centre.
Yo también quiero un hotel de cuatro estrellas.	I also want a four-star hotel.
Los dos queremos un hotel de cuatro estrellas.	We both want a four-star hotel.

Querer also means "to love". *Te quiero.* – I love you.

"Hay"

The impersonal form **hay** does not change in the present tense.

Example:

Hay un hotel de cinco estrellas y hay trece hoteles de cuatro estrellas.	There is a five-star hotel and there are 13 four-star hotels.

Hay cannot however be translated by "there is / there are" in every situation. For example
  Hay café means
  "There is coffee there" or "I/We have coffee".

In Spanish shops, hotels or restaurants you might see the following notices.

HAY CARNE DE LIDIA	Bull-fight meat for sale
HAY LOTERIA DE NAVIDAD	Christmas lottery tickets for sale
NO HAY ENTRADAS	No tickets for sale
NO HAY HABITACIONES LIBRES	No vacancies
NO HAY SALIDA	No exit

"Ir a hacer algo"

The form *vamos a* + **infinitive** is often used to make a suggestion.

Examples:
Francisco:

Vamos a reservar dos habitaciones dos noches.	Let's reserve two rooms for two nights.
Vamos a desayunar.	Let's have breakfast.
Vamos a tomar café.	Let's drink a coffee.

The Verb *ir* (to go) is Conjugated Irregularly:

		IR (Present)
	1. Pers.	*voy*
Singular	2. Pers.	*vas*
	3. Pers.	*va*
	1. Pers.	*vamos*
Plural	2. Pers.	*vais*
	3. Pers.	*van*

The form *ir a hacer algo* (literally: to be going to do something) can be interpreted in two ways:

1. *ir a hacer algo*   I am going to dance.
   Voy a bailar.

2. *ir a hacer algo*   I will dance.
   Voy a bailar.

Examples:

Vamos a ir a Madrid.	We will go to Madrid.
Voy a tomar café.	I will drink coffee.

The Negation

No means "no" as well as "not". When negating a sentence the particle *no* comes before the verb.

Examples:

¿Hay hoteles de seis estrellas?	Are there any six-star hotels?
No, no hay hoteles de seis estrellas.	No, there aren't any six-star hotels.
Alfonso no vive en Málaga.	Alfonso does not live in Málaga.
¿Quieres tomar un café?	Would you like to drink a coffee?
No, gracias.	No, thank you.

The Gender of the Noun

Almost all nouns which end in *-a* are feminine:

la tostada	la estrella
la ducha	la peseta

(one of the few exceptions is: el mapa)

Most nouns which end in *-o* are masculine:

el banco	el curso
el bocadillo	el teléfono

If the noun describes a person then the gender of the person is always the decisive factor irrespective of noun ending. Some words used to describe people can be used with both the masculine and the feminine article without modifying the form of the word, for example:

el policía (lthe policeman)	*la policía* (the policewoman)
el estudiante (the [male] student)	*la estudiante* (the [female] student)
el guía (the [male] guide)	*la guía* (the [female] guide

Nouns ending in *-ción* are always feminine:

la habitación   la calefacción

The Plural Form of the Noun

The plural form of Spanish nouns is extremely simple. Apart from a very small number of exceptions which we will discuss at the appropriate point, the plural of all nouns is formed by adding an *–s* when the noun ends with a vowel and an *–es* when it ends with a consonant.

Examples:

Nouns ending with a vowel:

Singular	Plural
estrella	estrellas
peseta	pesetas
bocadillo	bocadillos

Nouns ending with a consonant:

Singular	Plural
hotel	hoteles
hostal	hostales
pensión	pensiones

The feminine article *la* changes to *las* in the plural and the masculine article *el* changes to *los*.

Singular	Plural
la estrella	las estrellas
el hotel	los hoteles

 In many areas where Spanish is spoken (e.g. Southern Spain, The Canary Islands and large parts of Latin-America) the final -*s* is not sounded. Here *los amigos* [los amigos] becomes ⇒ [loamigo].

The Alphabet

As the Spanish find foreign names very difficult to write it is advisable to be able to spell your name. The Spanish alphabet is different to the English alphabet.

a	*a*
b	*be*
c	*ce*
ch	*che*
d	*de*
e	*e*
f	*efe*
g	*ge*
h	*hache*
i	*i*
j	*jota*
k	*ka*
l	*ele*
ll	*elle*
m	*eme*
n	*ene*
ñ	*eñe*
o	*o*
p	*pe*
q	*qu*
r	*erre*
s	*ese*

t	te
u	u
v	uve
w	uve doble
x	ekis
y	i griega
z	zeta

The Spanish alphabet has three more letters than the English alphabet. These are ch, ll and ñ.

Supplementary Exercise 1

Who is this?

1. jota, u, ele, i, o i, ge, ele, e, ese, i, a, ese

2. a, ene, te, o, ene, i, o be, a, ene, de, e, erre, a, ese

3. te, o, ene, i griega, b, ele, a, i, ere

Information about the Country

Hotels and Guest Houses

A Spanish *hotel* is the equivalent of a British Hotel. A *hostal* is a type of small hotel which is not quite as comfortable as a hotel. The Spanish *pensión* is similar to a British guest house or boarding house. Nowadays the *hostal* and the *pensión* are equivalent in many places.

People's Names

Nearly all of the Spanish have two surnames. The first they get from their father and the second from their mother. Unlike in Britain, the name is not relinquished after marrying. This can result in some pretty amazing combinations such as the following:

El hijo de Felipe González Márquez y Carmen Romero López se llama Pablo González Romero.
La hija de Antonio Ruiz Lozano y Estrella García Molero se llama Miriam Ruiz García.

Solution to the Supplementary Exercise

1. Julio Iglesias
2. Antonio Banderas
3. Tony Blair

LECCIÓN 4

De turismo en Granada

In this lesson you will learn how to:

- say what the date is
- enquire about other people's opinions
- formulate your own opinion
- agree to a suggestion or reject a suggestion

CD1
TOP 16 Remember the following phrases:

¿Hay algún restaurante cerca?	Is there a restaurant nearby?
un restaurante típico	a typical restaurant
por supuesto	of course
hay muchísimos	there are a lot
un restaurante de cuatro tenedores	a restaurant with four forks (four-star)
la estación de trenes	the railway station
¿Está lejos?	Is it far?
Está cerca.	It is nearby.
No es barato.	It is not cheap.
¿No hay restaurantes más	Aren't there any more reasonably-priced restaurants?
Aquí tiene.	Here, please.
muchas gracias - de nada	many thanks – you're welcome
muchas gracias - no hay de qué	many thanks – don't mention it
¿Qué vamos a hacer mañana?	What are we going to do tomorrow?
¿Qué quieres hacer?	What would you like to do?
¿Qué te parece? - Me parece muy bien.	What do you think about that? – I think it's good.

¿A qué hora salimos?	What time shall we leave?
a las nueve y media	at half past nine
una visita guiada a la ciudad	a guided tour of the city
El autobús sale a las nueve.	The bus leaves at 9 o'clock.
de acuerdo	agreed
vale	OK
hasta mañana	until (see you) tomorrow
Quiero visitar la ciudad.	I want to see the city (literally "visit")
Prefiero ir al campo.	I prefer to go into the country.
pasado mañana	the day after tomorrow

Los meses del año:	**The Months of the Year:**
enero	January
febrero	February
marzo	March
abril	April
mayo	May
junio	June
julio	July
agosto	August
septiembre	September
octubre	October
noviembre	November
diciembre	December

A: DIÁLOGOS

The story:
After arriving at the hotel Alfonso and Francisco get further information about the area from the receptionist.

Receptionist
¿Desean ustedes cenar en el hotel esta noche?

Would you like to eat dinner at the hotel this evening?

Alfonso
No, no, queremos cenar en un restaurante típico granadino. ¿Hay alguno cerca?

No, no, we would like to have dinner in a typical restaurant of Granada. Is there one nearby?

Receptionist
Sí, por supuesto, hay muchísimos. Hay un restaurante de cuatro tenedores cerca de la Alhambra. Es excelente, pero no es barato.

Yes of course, there are a lot. There is a "four-fork" restaurant near the Alhambra. It is excellent but not cheap.

Francisco
Un restaurante de cuatro tenedores es demasiado caro. ¿No hay restaurantes más económicos?

A "four-fork" restaurant is too expensive. Aren't there any more reasonably priced restaurants?

Receptionist
Cerca de la estación de trenes hay varios más económicos, pero muy buenos.

Near the railway station there are several which are more reasonable but very good.

Francisco
¿Está lejos, la estación de trenes?

Is the railway station far?

Receptionist
No, está bastante cerca. Aquí tiene un mapa de Granada. Nosotros estamos aquí y la estación de trenes está aquí.

No, it is quite near. Here have (take) a street-map of Granada. We are here and the railway station is here.

Francisco
Muchas gracias.

Many thanks.

Receptionist
De nada. Aquí tiene las llaves.

Your're welcome. Here are your keys.

Francisco
Muchas gracias.

Many thanks.

Receptionist
No hay de qué.

Don't mention it.

Alfonso and Francisco
Adiós y buenas tardes.

Goodbye and have a pleasant evening.

Receptionist
Muy buenas tardes.

Thank you, and the same to you.

The story:
Alfonso and Francisco are planning their weekend in Granada.

Alfonso
Bueno, amigo mío, ¿qué vamos a hacer mañana? En Granada hay muchísimas posibilidades. ¿Quieres visitar la ciudad o prefieres ir al campo?

Now, my friend what are we going to do tomorrow. In Granada there are a lot of possibilities. Do you want to see the city or would you prefer to go into the country?

Francisco
Por supuesto que quiero visitar la ciudad. Quiero ver la Alhambra y tambiénquiero visitar la ciudad antigua. Y tú, ¿qué quieres hacer?

I want to see the city of course. I want to see the Alhambra and also visit the old part of the city. And you, what do you want to do?

Alfonso
Me gusta mucho la naturaleza y en Granada hay de todo. Hay montañas y hay playa. Quiero visitar la costa de Granada. Es famosa por su clima agradable y sus frutas tropicales.

I love nature and in Granada there is everything. There are mountains and there is the beach. I would like to see the coast of Granada. It is famous for its pleasant climate and its tropical fruit.

Francisco
Vale, tenemos dos días, uno para visitar la ciudad de Granada y otro para ver la costa; mañana la ciudad y pasado mañana la costa. ¿Qué te parece?

OK, we have two days, one to see the city of Granada and one to see the coast; tomorow the city and the day after tomorrow the coast. What do you think of that?

Alfonso
Muy bien. ¿A qué hora salimos?

Great, what time shall we leave?

Francisco
Podemos desayunar a las nueve en el hotel y después hacemos una visita guiada a la ciudad. El autobús sale a las nueve y media del hotel.

We can have breakfast at nine in the hotel and afterwards we will go on guided tour of the city. The bus leaves at half past nine from the hotel.

Alfonso
De acuerdo. A las nueve en el restaurante del hotel. Hasta mañana entonces y buenas noches.

Agreed. At nine o'clock in the hotel restaurant. So see you tomorrow and good night.

Francisco
Buenas noches.

Good night.

B: EJERCICIOS

 Ejercicio 1:

Pregunte dónde hay algo bueno – Ask for something using the word good.

E **Ejemplo – Example:**

Voz: *un restaurante*

Usted: *¿Dónde hay un restaurante bueno?*
         Where is there a good restaurant?

Voz: *¿Dónde hay un restaurante bueno?*

Usted: *¿Dónde hay un restaurante bueno?*

 Y ahora usted, por favor – and now you:

1. un restaurante
   ¿Dónde hay un restaurante bueno?   Where is there a good restaurant?

2. una pensión
   ¿Dónde hay una pensión buena?   Where is there a good guest house?

3. Hoteles
   ¿Dónde hay hoteles buenos?   Where are there some good hotels?

4. Churros
   ¿Dónde hay churros buenos?   Where are there some good "Churros"?

65

5. Tostadas
¿Dónde hay tostadas buenas?   Where can you get some good toast?

6. Tomates
¿Dónde hay tomates buenos?   Where can you get good tomatoes?

7. Café
¿Dónde hay una cafetería buena?   Where can you get some good coffee?

 Ejercicio 2:
CD1 TOP19

Responda siempre que más – Reply using the comparative form (better, larger etc.)

E Ejemplo – Example:

Voz: *El Hotel Meliá es caro. ¿Y el Hotel La Bobadilla?*
Hotel Meliá is expensive. And Hotel La Bobadilla?

Usted: *El Hotel La Bobadilla es más caro.*
La Bobadilla is more expensive.

Voz: *El Hotel La Bobadilla es más caro.*

Usted: *El Hotel La Bobadilla es más caro.*

Y ahora usted, por favor – and now you:

1. El Hotel Meliá es caro.
   ¿Y el Hotel La Bobadilla?
   El Hotel La Bobadilla es más caro.

   The Meliá hotel is expensive.
   And the La Bobadilla hotel?
   The La Bobadilla hotel is more
   expensive.

2. La Pensión Luna es económica.
   ¿Y la Pensión Sol?
   La Pensión Sol es más económica.

   The Luna guest house is reasonable
   And the Sol guest house?
   The Sol guest house is more reasonable.

3. Los restaurantes de tres tenedores
   son buenos. ¿Y los restaurantes de
   cuatro tenedores?
   Los restaurantes de cuatro tenedores
   son mejores.

   Three-fork restaurants are
   good. And four-fork
   restaurants?
   Four-fork restaurants are better.

4. Conchi y Clara son guías típicas.
   ¿Y Rosa y María?
   Rosa y María son más típicas.

   Conchi and Clara are typical tour
   guides. And Rosa and María?
   Rosa and María are more typical.

5. La estación de trenes está lejos.
   ¿Y la estación de autobuses?
   La estación de autobuses está más
   lejos.

   The railway station is far away.
   And the bus station?
   The bus station is further away.

6. El Café Central es caro.
   ¿Y el Café Royal?
   El Café Royal es más caro.

   The Café Central is expensive.
   And the Café Royal?
   The Café Royal is more expensive.

7. El Hostal Roca es malo ¿Y el Hostal
   Arena? El Hostal Arena es peor.

   The Hostal Roca is bad.
   And the Hostal Arena?
   The Hostal Arena ist worse.

Ejercicio 3:
Diga que sí le gusta. – Say that you like it.

E Ejemplo – Example:

Voz: *¿Te gusta la naturaleza?*
           Do you like nature?

Usted: *Sí, me gusta la naturaleza.*
           Yes, I like nature.

Voz: *Sí, me gusta la naturaleza.*

Usted: *Sí, me gusta la naturaleza.*

 Y ahora usted, por favor – and now you:

1. ¿Te gusta la naturaleza?   Do you like nature?
   Sí, me gusta la naturaleza.   Yes, I like nature.

2. ¿Y la playa?
   Sí, me gusta la playa.   Yes, I like the beach.

3. ¿Y las montañas?
   Sí, me gustan las montañas.   Yes, I like the mountains.

4. ¿Y los hoteles de cuatro estrellas?
   Sí, me gustan los hoteles de cuatro   Yes, I like four-star hotels.
   estrellas.

5. ¿Y los toros?
   Sí, me gustan los toros.   Yes, I like bullfights.

6. ¿Y las frutas tropicales?
   Sí, me gustan las frutas tropicales.   Yes, I like tropical fruit.

7. ¿Y la ciudad de Granada?
   Si, me gusta la ciudad de Granada.   Yes, I like the city of Granada.

^{CD1}_{TOP21} **Ejercicio 4:**
Responda – Answer the question.

 Ejemplo – Example:

    Voz: *¿Se puede esquiar en Sierra Nevada?*
               Can you ski in the Sierra Nevada?

    Usted: *Sí, se puede esquiar en Sierra Nevada.*
               Yes, you can ski in the Sierra Nevada.

    Voz: *Sí, se puede esquiar en Sierra Nevada.*

    Usted: *Sí, se puede esquiar en Sierra Nevada.*

Y ahora usted, por favor – and now you:

1. ¿Se puede esquiar en Sierra Nevada?
   Sí, se puede esquiar en Sierra
   Nevada.

   Can you ski in the Sierra Nevada?
   Yes, you can ski in the Sierra Nevada.

2. ¿Se puede caminar en los Pirineos?
   Sí, se puede caminar en los Pirineos.

   Can you go walking in the Pyrenees
   Yes, you can go walking in the
   Pyrenees.

3. ¿Se puede hacer una visita guiada a
   la ciudad de Granada?
   Sí, se puede hacer una visita guiada
   a la ciudad de Granada.

   Can you go on a guided tour
   of the city in Granada?
   Yes, you can go on a guided tour
   of the city in Granada.

4. ¿Se puede visitar la Alhambra?
   Sí, se puede visitar la Alhambra.

   Can you visit the Alhambra?
   Yes, you can visit the Alhambra.

5. ¿Se puede cenar en el Hotel Meliá?
   Sí, se puede cenar en el Hotel Meliá.

   Can you have dinner in the Hotel Meliá?
   Yes, you can have dinner in the Hotel
   Meliá.

6. ¿Se puede desayunar en el hotel
   a las ocho de la mañana?
   Sí, se puede desayunar en el hotel
   a las ocho de la mañana.

   Can you have breakfast in the hotel
   at 8 o'clock?
   Yes you can have breakfast in the
   hotel at 8 o'clock.

7. ¿Se puede fumar aquí?
   Sí, aquí se puede fumar.

   Is smoking allowed here?
   Yes, smoking is allowed here.

GRAMÁTICA

The Date

In Spanish the date is formed as follows:

Number + *de* + **Month**

e.g. *veintitrés de mayo*

Example:

Alfonso y Francisco están en Granada los días veintitrés y veinticuatro de mayo.	Alfonso and Francisco are in Granada on the 23rd and 24th of May.

In Spanish years are treated the same way as normal numbers. Instead of saying nineteen ninety-seven you say one thousand nine hundred and ninety-seven.
mil novecientos noventa y siete.

Examples:
1997 – *mil novecientos noventa y siete*
1998 – *mil novecientos noventa y ocho*
1989 – *mil novecientos ochenta y nueve*
1492 – *mil cuatrocientos noventa y dos*

Use the following construction to say the date in full:

Number + *de* + **Month** + *de* + **Year**

e.g. *once de octubre de mil novecientos noventa y siete*

¿Qué día es hoy?	What's today's date?
Hoy es once de octubre de mil novecientos noventa y siete.	Today is 11th of October 1997.

Supplementary Exercise 1

Say the Date.

Example:
¿Qué día es hoy? (25th November 1997)
Hoy es veinticinco de noviembre de mil novecientos noventa y siete.

1. 25th November 1997;
2. 31st March 1997;
3   9th October 1998;
4. 1st January 2000.

Querer vs. desear

The verb **desear** is more polite than the simpler **querer** and is used more frequently for formal occasions. It is used most commonly in phrases such as: **¿Qué desean los señores?** – What would you gentlemen like?

Example:

recepcionista:
¿Desean ustedes cenar en el hotel esta noche?

Do you wish to have dinner in the hotel this evening?

The receptionist could also have asked
¿Quieren ustedes cenar en el hotel esta noche?

Would you like to have dinner in the hotel this evening?

The Adjective

Unlike English, the adjective normally comes after the noun.

un restaurante típico

The adjective also changes its ending depending on whether the noun is masculine or feminine. (We have already seen this phenomenen when using multiples of a hundred).

el restaurante típico

but

la secretaria típica

If the noun is in the plural then the adjective has the plural -*s* ending.

Example:

el estudiante típico the typical student
la guía típica the typical (female) tour guide
los hoteles típicos the typical hotels
las pensiones típicas the typical guest houses

The Comparative

The comparative form for adjectives and adverbs is formed by simply preceding the word with *más* :

económico	cheap
***más** económico*	cheaper (literally: more cheap)

Examples:

más caro	more expensive
más cerca	nearer
más lejos	further
más típico	more typical

Some important irregular forms:

bueno	*mejor*
malo	*peor*

Examples:

El Hotel Reina Ana es bueno.	*El Hotel Reina Sofía es mejor.*
Madrid es cara.	*San Sebastián es más cara.*
Córdoba está cerca de Madrid.	*Jaén está más cerca de Madrid.*
El café solo es bueno.	*El café con leche es mejor.*

The form **muchísimo** is the superlative of **mucho** and expresses the fact that something exists in the largest possible quantity or to the highest possible degree.
recepcionista:

Hay muchísimos restaurantes.	There are an awful lot of restaurants.

For this reason it is a good idea only to use those forms which you have heard in the original or seen in print.

Note: The word *mucho* can be used as an adverb as well as an adjective. As an adverb, *mucho* always has the same form:
*Me alegro **mucho** de veros.*

On the other hand, as an adjective, the endings of *mucho* and also of the superlative form **muchísimo**, agree with the noun as do all other adjectives:
mucho queso
muchísimo queso
mucha mantequilla
muchísima mantequilla
muchos restaurantes
muchísimos restaurantes
muchas habitaciones
muchísimas habitaciones

The Verb „preferir"

The conjugation of the verb **preferir** deviates in part from the standard pattern. In the singular and the third person plural the root vowel is modified.

		PREFERIR (Present)
	1. Pers.	*prefiero*
Singular	2. Pers.	*prefieres*
	3. Pers.	*prefiere*
	1. Pers.	*preferimos*
Plural	2. Pers.	*preferís*
	3. Pers.	*prefieren*

Preferir literally translated means "to prefer to do something". In most cases the translation "to rather do something" is more suitable.

Example:

¿Quieres visitar la ciudad o prefieres ir al campo?	Do you want to see the city or would you rather go into the country?
Prefiero ir al campo.	I would rather go into the country.

Supplementary Exercise 2
What would you rather do or have?

Example: ¿Quiere tomar café o té? – Prefiero tomar café.

1. ¿Quiere tomar café o tomar té?
2. ¿Quiere ir a Madrid o a Mallorca?
3. ¿Quiere un hotel de cuatro estrellas o una pensión?
4. ¿Quiere cenar en un restaurante caro o en un restaurante económico?

"Me gusta"

gustar	to like
me gusta	"I like"
me gusta mucho	"I like something a lot" or also "I love something"

Example:

Alfonso: _Me gusta mucho la naturaleza._ – I love nature.

If you are talking about more than one thing which you like then the verb **gustar** is used in the plural.

Examples:

Me gustan los hoteles de cuatro estrellas.	I like four-start hotels.
No me gustan las pensiones.	I don't like guest houses.
Me gustan los toros.	I like bullfights.

(_Los toros_ means literally the bulls. It is also used when bullfight is meant.)

"Gustar" can also be used in conjunction with a verb:

me gusta bailar	I love to dance.

Examples:

Me gusta cenar con amigos.	I like eating dinner with friends.
No me gusta vivir en la ciudad.	I don't like living in the city.
Me gusta vivir en el campo.	I like living in the country.

The Superlative

In Spanish, the superlative is formed in the same way as the comparative:

la montaña más alta	the highest mountain.

The forms are often ambiguous and in many cases their meaning is only obvious from the context.

Examples:

El Teide es la montaña más alta de España. Tiene 3718 metros de altura. El Teide es un volcán.

El Mulhacén de Sierra Nevada es la montaña más alta de la Península Ibérica. Tiene 3481 metros de altura.

La montaña más alta de Francia es el Mont-Blanc. Tiene 4807 metros de altura.

El Everest es la montaña más alta del mundo. Tiene 8848 metros de altura.

Supplementary Exercise 3
Proceed as in the following example.

Example: El Everest; El Everest es la montaña más alta del mundo.
1. El Everest;
2. El Mulhacén;
3. El Teide;
4. El Zugspitze.

The Verb "poder"

The conjugation of the modal verb **poder** also deviates in part from the standard pattern. In the singular and the third person plural the root vowel is modified.

PODER (Present)

	1. Pers.	*puedo*
Singular	2. Pers.	*puedes*
	3. Pers.	*puede*
	1. Pers.	*podemos*
Plural	2. Pers.	*podéis*
	3. Pers.	*pueden*

Examples:

Podemos desayunar a las nueve en el hotel.	We can have breakfast at nine o'clock in the hotel.
¿Qué podemos hacer?	What can we do?
Podemos visitar la ciudad.	We can see the city.
Podemos ir al campo.	We can go into the country.
Podemos ir a las montañas.	We can go to the mountains.
Podemos ir a la playa.	We can go to the beach.

The impersonal form *"se puede"* always has the same form when it used with a verb.

se puede	you/one can
se puede caminar	you/one can go walking
se puede esquiar	you/one can go skiing

Examples:

En Sierra Nevada se puede caminar.	In the Sierra Nevada you can go walking.
En Sierra Nevada se puede esquiar.	In the Sierra Nevada you can ski.
En los Pirineos se puede caminar y esquiar.	In the Pyrenees you can go walking and skiing.
En el Teide se puede caminar, pero no se puede esquiar.	On Teide you can go walking but not skiing.
En el Everest no se puede ni caminar ni esquiar.	On Everest you can neither go walking nor skiing.

The impersonal form *¿Se puede?* is also frequently used to ask permission before entering a room.

Knock	
Sí	Yes?
- ¿Se puede?	May I (one) enter?
- ¿Adelante!	Yes, please! (come in!)

The Verb "hacer"

The verb *hacer* (to do) is conjugated irregularly. But in the present tense only the first person singular is irregular.

HACER (Present)		
	1. Pers.	*hago*
Singular	2. Pers.	*haces*
	3. Pers.	*hace*
	1. Pers.	*hacemos*
Plural	2. Pers.	*hacéis*
	3. Pers.	*hacen*

Examples:

Nosotros hacemos una visita guiada a la ciudad.	We take part in a guided tour of the city. (do a guided tour of the city)
Carmen y Mónica hacen una visita guiada a Sierra Nevada.	Carmen and Monika take part in a guided tour of the Sierra Nevada.
Juan hace una visita guiada a la Costa del Sol.	Juan takes part in a sightseeing tour of the Costa del Sol.
Felipe hace una visita guiada al Museo.	Felipe takes part in a guided tour of the museum.
Y usted, ¿qué visita hace usted?	And you, what sort of guided tour are you going to take part in?

Asking an Opinion

A common phrase used to enquire of someone's opinion about something is *"qué te parece"*.

Examples:

¿Qué te parece?	What do you think (of that)?
¿Qué le parece?	What do they think?
¿Qué os parece?	What do you (plural) think?
or just:	
Me parece bien.	I think it's good (a good idea).
Me parece mal.	I think it's bad (a bad idea).

or just:

bien	good
muy bien	very good
mal	bad
muy mal	very bad

Example:

Francisco: *Un día visitamos la ciudad y otro vamos al campo, ¿qué te parece?*
Alfonso: *Me parece muy bien.*

Visitamos la ciudad de Granada. ¿Qué le parece? – Me parece muy bien.
Tomamos un bocadillo de queso. ¿Qué le parece? – Me parece muy bien.
Vamos a la playa. ¿Qué le parece? – Me parece muy bien.
Vamos a bailar a una discoteca. ¿Qué le parece? -– Me parece muy bien.

Another phrase which is used very often to agree to a suggestion is
de acuerdo (agreed).

Francisco: *Podemos desayunar a las nueve en el hotel y después hacemos una visita guiada a la ciudad. El autobús sale a las 9 y media del hotel.*

Alfonso: *De acuerdo.*

An even more common form of agreement which is very colloquial is **vale**.

Vamos a bailar a una discoteca.
Vale.

Information about the Country

Spain is divided into 17 regions, the so-called *comunidades autónomas*, and into 50 provinces, *las provincias*, each of which has its own provincial capital. In most cases the name of the province is the same as the name of its capital, meaning that you must clearly indicate whether you mean the city or the province.

Examples:

la ciudad de Granada	– la provincia de Granada
la ciudad de Madrid	– la provincia de Madrid
la ciudad de Valencia	– la provincia de Valencia
la ciudad de Barcelona	– la provincia de Barcelona
la ciudad de Toledo	– la provincia de Toledo

and so on.

Supplementary Exercise 4

Translate the Following:

En Granada hay de todo.
En Granada hay montañas. Las montañas de Granada se llaman Sierra Nevada.
En Granada hay costa. La costa de Granada se llama Costa Tropical.
En la Costa del Sol hay muchas playas.

En Gerona también hay de todo.
En Gerona hay montañas. Las montañas de Gerona se llaman Los Pirineos.
En Gerona hay costa. La costa de Gerona se llama Costa Brava.
En la Costa Brava hay muchas playas.

En España hay muchas montañas. Las montañas más importantes son Los Pirineos, Sierra Nevada y el Teide. Los Pirineos están en el norte de España. Sierra Nevada está en el sur de España. El Teide está en la isla de Tenerife.

en el norte de	in the north of
en el sur de	in the south of

Supplementary Exercise 5
Say where the following mountains are located.

Example: los Pirineos; Los Pirineos están en el norte de España.

1. los Pirineos;
2. Sierra Nevada;
3. el Mont-Blanc;
4. el Teide.

Solutions to the Supplementary Exercises

Supplementary Exercise 1

1. Hoy es 25 de noviembre de mil novecientos noventa y siete.
2. Hoy es treinta y uno de marzo de mil novecientos noventa y siete.
3. Hoy es nueve de octubre de mil novecientos noventa y ocho.
4. Hoy es uno de enero del año dos mil.

Supplementary Exercise 3

1. El Everest es la montaña más alta del mundo.
2. El Mulhacén es la montaña más alta de la Península Ibérica.
3. El Teide es la montaña más alta de España.
4. El Zugspitze es la montaña más alta de Alemania.

Supplementary Exercise 4

Granada has everything.
In Granada there are mountains. The mountains of Granada are called the Sierra Nevada.
In Granada there is a coast. The coast of Granada is called the Costa del Sol.
On the Costa del Sol there are a lot of beaches.

Gerona has everything.
In Gerona there are mountains. The mountains of Gerona are called the Pyrenees.
In Gerona there is a coast. The coast of Gerona is called the Costa Brava.
On the Costa Brava there are a lot of beaches.

In Spain there are a lot of mountains. The most important mountains are the Pyrenees, the Sierra Nevada and Teide. The Pyrenees are in the north of Spain. The Sierra Nevada is in the south of Spain. Teide is on the island of Tenerife.

Supplementary Exercise 5

1. Los Pirineos están en el norte de España.
2. Sierra Nevada está en el sur de España.
3. El Zugspitze está en el sur de Alemania.
4. El Teide está en la isla de Tenerife.

Planeando el fin de semana

LECCIÓN 5

In this lesson you will learn how to:

- ask where something is
- say where something is
- order in a restaurant

CD2
TOP 1 Remember the following phrases:

¡Qué ciudad más bonita!	What a lovely city!
¡Qué cansado estoy!	How tired I am!
Vamos a comer algo.	Let's eat something.
Tengo hambre.	I am hungry.
¿Dónde hay un restaurante por aquí cerca?	Where is there a restaurant here in the vicinity?
Hay muchos.	There are a lot.
al final de la calle	at the end of the road
a la derecha o a mano derecha	on the right; on the right-hand side
a la izquierda o a mano izquierda	on the left; on the left-hand side
en la plaza	in the square
Es muy bueno.	It is very good.
No es barato.	It is not cheap.
muchas gracias - de nada	many thanks – don't mention it
un restaurante italiano	an Italian restaurant
un restaurante español	a Spanish restaurant
un plato típico	a typical dish
Me encanta.	I love it.
Es igual.	It doesn't matter.

bacalao a la vizcaína	Biscay-style cod
la especialidad de la casa	the house speciality
naturalmente	naturally, of course
una ensalada mixta	a mixed salad
vino blanco de la casa	house white (wine)
agua mineral con gas	carbonated mineral water
agua mineral sin gas	still mineral water

A: DIÁLOGOS

The story: Alfonso and Francisco have just completed their tour of the city:

Alfonso
¡Qué ciudad más bonita!

What a lovely city!

Francisco
¡Y qué cansado estoy! Anda, vamos a comer algo. Tengo hambre.

And how tired I am! Come on, let's eat something. I'm hungry.

Alfonso
Sí, sí, muy bien, yo también quiero comer algo. Vamos a preguntar dónde hay un restaurante por aquí. (...) Perdone, Señor, ¿dónde hay un restaurante por aquí cerca?

Yes, OK, I also want to eat something. Let's ask where there's a restaurant here. (...) Excuse me, Señor, where is there a restaurant here in the vicinity?

Man
Aquí hay muchos restaurantes. Al final de la calle, a la derecha, hay un restaurante italiano. Y un poco más lejos también hay un restaurante chino.

There are a lot of restaurants here. At the end of the road on the right-hand side there is an Italian restaurant. And a little further on there is also a Chinese restaurant.

Alfonso
Preferimos un restaurante español.

We would prefer a Spanish restaurant.

Man
Un restaurante español. Hay uno en la plaza a mano izquierda. Es muy bueno, pero no es barato.

There is one in the square on the left-hand side. It is good, but not cheap.

85

Francisco
Muchas gracias.   Many thanks.

Man
De nada.   Don't mention it.

The story: Alfonso and Francisco are in the restaurant.

Waiter
Buenas tardes.   Good evening.

Alfonso und Francisco
Buenas tardes.   Good evening.

Waiter
¿Qué desean tomar?   What would you like? (to eat/drink)

Alfonso
Queremos comer un plato típico
español.   We would like to eat a typical Spanish dish.

Waiter
¿De carne o de pescado?   Meat or fish?

Alfonso
Es igual, de carne o de pescado,
a mí me encanta el pescado pero
también me gusta mucho la carne,
¿y a ti?   It doesn't matter, meat or fish. I love fish, but I also like meat. And you?

Francisco
Yo prefiero comer pescado.
En España el pescado es muy bueno.
¿Qué pescado hay?   I prefer fish. In Spain the fish is very good. What sort of fish do you have?

Waiter
Tenemos bacalao a la vizcaína que es
muy bueno. Hay merluza, boquerones,
calamares, gambas y naturalmente
hay paella. Es la especialidad de la casa.   We have Biscay-style cod. It is very good. We have hake, anchovies, octopus rings, prawns and of course paella. It is the house speciality.

Alfonso
Ah, sí, yo quiero paella.   Oh, yes, I would like paella.

Francisco
Y yo también, y una ensalada mixta.

And the same for me, and a
mixed salad.

Waiter
Una paella para dos, una ensalada
mixta, ¿y para beber?

A paella for two, a mixed salad;
and (something) to drink?

Francisco
¿Tomamos vino blanco?

Shall we have white wine?

Alfonso
Sí, vino blanco de la casa y agua
mineral.

Yes, the house white and some
mineral water.

Waiter
Agua mineral, ¿con o sin gas?

The mineral water: carbonated or still?

Alfonso
Sin gas, por favor.

Still, please.

Waiter
Muy bien, vino blanco de la casa y
agua nineral sin gas.

So that's, the house white and some
still mineral water.

EJERCICIOS

 Ejercicio 1:
„¡Qué bonito!"

E Ejemplo – Example:

Voz: *la ciudad*

Usted: *¡Qué ciudad más bonita!*

         What a lovely city!

Voz: *¡Qué ciudad más bonita!*

Usted: *¡Qué ciudad más bonita!*

 Y ahora usted, por favor – and now you:

1. Ciudad
   ¡Qué ciudad más bonita!   What a lovely city!

2. Hotel
   ¡Qué hotel más bonito!   What a lovely hotel!

3. Habitaciones
   ¡Qué habitaciones más bonitas!   What lovely rooms!

4. Baño
   ¡Qué baño más bonito!   What a lovely bathroom!

5. playas
   ¡Qué playas más bonitas!   What lovely beaches!

6. plaza
   ¡Qué plaza más bonita!   What a lovely square!

7. visita
   ¡Qué visita más bonita!   What a lovely sight-seeing tour!

Ejercicio 2:
Pregunte dónde – Ask where something is.

E Ejemplo – Example:

Voz: *un restaurante italiano*

Usted: *¿Dónde hay un restaurante italiano?*
Where is there an Italian restaurant?

Voz: *¿Dónde hay un restaurante italiano?*

Usted: *¿Dónde hay un restaurante italiano?*

 Y ahora usted, por favor – and now you:

1. un restaurante italiano
   ¿Dónde hay un restaurante italiano? Where is there an Italian restaurant?

2. la ciudad antigua
   ¿Dónde está la ciudad antigua? Where is the old part of the city?

3. la estación de autobuses
   ¿Dónde está la estación de Where is the bus station?
   autobuses?

4. un médico
   ¿Dónde hay un médico? Where is there a doctor?

5. una farmacia
   ¿Dónde hay una farmacia? Where is there a pharmacy?

6. la oficina de turismo
¿Dónde está la oficina de turismo?   Where is the tourist office?

7. los servicios
¿Dónde están los servicios?   Where are the toilets?

 Ejercicio 3:
Repita donde está – Repeat where something is.

E Ejemplo – Example:

Voz: *Al final de la calle, a la derecha, hay un restaurante italiano.*
At the end of the road, on the right, there is an Italian
restaurant.

Otra voz: *¿Dónde?*
Who?

Usted: *Al final de la calle, a la derecha.*
At the end of the road, on the right.

Voz: *Al final de la calle, a la derecha.*

Usted: *Al final de la calle, a la derecha.*

Y ahora usted, por favor – and now you:

1. – Al final de la calle, a la derecha, hay un restaurante italiano.
   – ¿Dónde?
   – Al final de la calle, a la derecha.

   – At the end of the road, on the right, there is an Italian restaurant.
   – Where?
   – At the end of the road, on the right.

2. – Un poco más lejos hay un restaurante chino.
   – ¿Dónde?
   – Un poco más lejos

   – A little further on there is a Chinese restaurant.
   – Where?
   – A little further on.

3. – Hay un restaurante español en la plaza, a mano izquierda.
   – ¿Dónde?
   – En la plaza, a mano izquierda.

   – There is a Spanish restaurant in the square, on the left-hand side
   – Where?
   – In the square, on the left-hand side.

4. – La farmacia está al final de la calle, en el cruce.
   – ¿Dónde?
   – Al final de la calle, en el cruce.

   – The pharmacy is at the end of the road, at the crossroads.
   – Where?
   – At the end of the road, at the crossroads.

5. – La oficina de turismo está todo recto, en la plaza, a mano derecha.
   – ¿Dónde?
   – Todo recto, en la plaza, a mano derecha.

   – The tourist office is straight ahead, in the square on the right-hand side.
   – Where?
   – Straight ahead, in the square on the right-hand side.

6. – Hay un médico en la tercera calle a la derecha.
   – ¿Dónde?
   – En la tercera calle a la derecha.

   – There is a doctor in the third street on the right.
   – Where?
   – In the third street on the right.

7. – El hospital está todo recto, en la segunda plaza.
   – ¿Dónde?
   – Todo recto, en la segunda plaza.

   – The hospital is straight ahead, in the second square.
   – Where?
   – Straight ahead, in the second square.

Ejercicio 4:

Responda que le gusta mucho – **Answer by saying that you like it.**

E Ejemplo – **Example:**

Voz: *¿Te gusta el vino blanco?*
Do you like white wine?

Usted: *Sí, me gusta mucho. Me encanta el vino blanco.*
Yes, very much. I love white wine.

Voz: *Sí, me gusta mucho.*
Me encanta el vino blanco.

Usted: *Sí, me gusta mucho.*
Me encanta el vino blanco.

 Y ahora usted, por favor – and now you:

1. ¿Te gusta el vino blanco?   Do you like white wine?
   Sí, me gusta mucho. Me encanta
   el vino blanco.

2. ¿Te gusta el bacalao a la vizcaína?   Do you like Biscay-style cod?
   Sí, me gusta mucho. Me encanta el
   bacalao a la vizcaína.

3. ¿Te gusta la ensalada mixta?   Do you like mixed salad?
   Sí, me gusta mucho. Me encanta la
   ensalada mixta.

4. ¿Te gusta la tostada con tomate   Do you like toast with tomato and oil?
   y aceite?
   Sí, me gusta mucho. Me encanta la
   tostada con tomate y aceite.

5. ¿Te gusta el pescado?   Do you like fish?
   Sí, me gusta mucho. Me encanta
   el pescado.

6. ¿Te gustan los boquerones?   Do you like anchovies?
   Sí, me gustan mucho. Me encantan
   los boquerones.

7. ¿Te gustan los calamares?   Do you like octopus rings?
   Sí, me gustan mucho. Me encantan
   los calamares.

GRAMÁTICA

Predicative Use of the Adjective

The endings of adjectives also agree with the noun when they are used in the predicative:

Examples:

Francisco: *¡Qué cansado estoy!*   How tired (or exhausted) I am!
If a woman had said this, she would have had to say:
¡Qué cansada estoy!
If Francisco and Alfonso had said this, they would have had to say:
¡Qué cansados estamos!
But if two women had said the same thing, they would have had to say:
¡Qué cansadas estamos!

Note: The feminine plural form is only used with the adjective when only referring to females (but not to males). Even if there is only one man amongst a number of women the adjective takes the masculine plural form:

Francisco y varias mujeres: *¡Qué cansados estamos!*

Supplementary Exercise 1
Form phrases of exclamation for the people mentioned.

Example:
> Ana; ¡Que cansada estoy!
> Ana;
> Ana y María;
> José;
> Ana y José.

Expression of a Physical State

Phrases such as "I'm hungry or thirsty", "I'm tired", "I'm hot" etc. which express a physical state are formed in Spanish using the verb tener + noun:

Examples:

Tengo hambre.	I'm hungry
Tengo sed.	I'm thirsty.
Tengo sueño.	I'm tired.
Tengo calor.	I'm hot.
Tengo frío.	I'm cold.

The Indefinite Article

The counterparts of the definite articles el and la are the indefinite articles
un and **una**:

el *restaurante*	**un** restaurante
la *ciudad*	**una** ciudad

If you want to ask generally about a hotel then use the indefinite article:
> ¿Dónde hay **un** hotel?   Where is there a hotel?

If, however, you want to ask about a particular hotel, then use the definite article:
> ¿Dónde está **el** Hotel Meliá?   Where is the Hotel Meliá?

In the first sentence the impersonal form *hay* was used and in the second
the verb *estar*:

> ¿Dónde **hay** un hotel?
> ¿Dónde **está** el Hotel Meliá?

Hay is used for a general question and the verb *estar* is used when you are asking
about something specific.

¿dónde hay?	Where is there ...?
¿dónde está?	Where is ...?

If the masculine indefinite article stands on its own, i.e. without the noun it refers
to, it is given the ending -*o: uno.*

> **un** restaurante español   BUT   hay **uno**

But the feminine indefinite article does not change.

> **una** habitación   AND   hay **una**

Example:

señor: *Un restaurante español. Hay uno en la plaza a mano izquierda.*
        A Spanish restaurant. There is one in the square on the left-hand side.

Supplementary Exercise 2

Answer the following questions using the indefinite article without the noun it refers to.

Example: ¿Hay un hotel por aquí cerca? – Sí, hay uno.

1. ¿Hay un hotel por aquí cerca?
2. ¿Hay una oficina de turismo por aquí cerca?
3. ¿Hay un médico por aquí cerca?
4. ¿Hay una farmacia por aquí cerca?

Describing the Way

al final de la calle	at the end of the road
al principio de la calle	at the beginning of the road
en la plaza	in the square

Examples:

El restaurante italiano está al final de la calle.
El restaurante chino está al principio de la calle.
El restaurante español está en la plaza.

a la derecha	OR	*a mano derecha* –	on the right; to the right on the right-hand side
a la izquierda	OR	*a mano izquierda* –	on the left; to the left; on the left-hand side

El restaurante italiano está al final de la calle, a la derecha OR a mano derecha.

El restaurante chino está al principio de la calle, a la izquierda OR a mano izquierda.

Other important expressions:

en el cruce	at the crossroads
todo recto	straight ahead

Supplementary Exercise 3

STREET MAP OF GRANADA

Look at the street map of Granada. You are in front of the post office. Various people ask you for information. Reply with the aid of the street map.

Example: ¿Dónde hay un banco por aquí cerca? – Hay uno al final de la calle, a la derecha.

1. ¿Dónde hay un banco por aquí cerca?
2. ¿Dónde está la oficina de turismo?
3. ¿Dónde hay una farmacia?
4. ¿Dónde está el hospital?

The Emphatic Personal Pronoun (Indirect Object and Direct Object)

In Spanish there are two types of personal pronouns: the dependent personal pronoun and the independent or emphatic personal pronoun. The dependent personal pronoun always comes next to the verb. The emphatic or independent personal pronoun can appear without the verb or in addition to the dependent personal pronoun to emphasise it.

Examples:

Me gusta el pescado.	I like fish.
	(literally: To me I like the fish.))
¿A tí?	You? (literally: to you?)
Sí, a mí.	Yes, I do (like fish).
	(literally: yes, to me.)

THE INDEPENDENT/EMPHATIC PERSONAL PRONOUN
(INDIRECT/DIRECT OBJECT)

	1. Pers.	**a mí**
Singular	2. Pers.	**a ti**
	3. Pers.	**a él/ella/usted**
	1. Pers.	**a nosotros**
Plural	2. Pers.	**a vosotros**
	3. Pers.	**a ellos/ellas/ustedes**

Examples:
Me encanta el pescado pero también me gusta mucho la carne.
¿Y a ti?
I love fish but I also like meat a lot. And you?
(literally: and to you?)
Me gusta la paella. ¿Y a usted?
I like paella. And you?

Solutions to the Supplementary Exercises

Supplementary Exercise 1

1. ¡Qué cansada estoy!
2. ¡Qué cansadas estamos!
3. ¡Qué cansado estoy!
4. ¡Qué cansados estamos!

Supplementary Exercise 2

1. Sí, hay uno.
2. Sí, hay una.
3. Sí, hay uno.
4. Sí, hay una.

Supplementary Exercise 3

1. Hay uno al final de la calle, a la derecha.
2. Está al final de la calle, en la plaza, a la derecha.
3. Hay una al principio de la calle, a la izquierda.
4. Está muy lejos de aquí.

LECCIÓN **6**

En casa de Doña María

In this lesson you will learn how to talk about the following subjects:

- the family
- tpersonal hygiene
- tschool

CD2 Remember the following phrases:
TOP7

en casa de doña María	at Doña Maria's house
Doña María es ama de casa.	Doña María is a housewife.
Está casada.	She is married.
Tiene tres hijos.	She has three children.
Miguel estudia en la universidad.	Miguel is at university (lit: studies at the university).
Dolores estudia bachillerato.	Dolores is at sixth-form college (is in the sixth-form).
Elena estudia educación primaria.	Elena is at primary school.
el más pequeño	the smallest (= the youngest)
No quiero tomar azúcar.	I don't want any sugar.
Estoy a régimen.	I am on a diet.
El autobús sale a las nueve.	The bus leaves at nine.
¿Dónde está Dolores?	Where is Dolores?
Es muy tarde.	It is very late.
Se marchan.	They go (on foot).

Los números ordinales:

primero	sexto
segundo	séptimo
tercero	octavo
cuarto	noveno
quinto	décimo

CD2
OP8

A: DIÁLOGOS

The story:
We meet Doña María from the first lesson again. Doña María is the mother of a large family.

The narrator

Estamos en casa de doña María.
Ella vive en Madrid, en la calle
Sagasta, número ocho, segundo B.
Doña María es ama de casa. Está
casada y tiene tres hijos: dos niñas
y un niño. Son las ocho de la
mañana. Doña María se levanta, se
ducha, se arregla y se viste.
Entonces despierta a Juan, su marido.

We are at Doña María's house.
She lives in Madrid at Sagasta Street,
number 8, on the second floor, flat B.
Doña María is a housewife. She
is married and has three children:
a girl and two boys. It is eight o'clock
in the morning. Doña María gets up,
showers, gets ready and dresses.
Then she wakes Juan, her husband.

The narrator continues:

Los hijos de doña María se llaman
Miguel, Dolores y Elena. Miguel tiene
19 años. Estudia en la universidad.
Dolores tiene 17 años y estudia
primero de bachillerato. Elena, la más
pequeña, tiene 8 años y estudia segundo de educación primaria. Doña
María despierta a su hijo Miguel.
Miguel se levanta, se ducha, se afeita
y se viste.Después, doña María también despierta a su hija Dolores. Ella
se levanta, se ducha, se maquilla y

The children of Doña María are called
Miguel, Dolores and Elena. Miguel
is 19 years old. He is at university.
Dolores is 17 and is in the first year of
the sixth form. Elena, the youngest,
is 8 and is in the second year of
primary school. Doña María
wakes her son Miguel. Miguel
gets up, showers, shaves and gets
dressed. Next Doña María wakes her
daughter Dolores. She gets up,
showers, puts on her makeup

se viste. También Elena se levanta.
Doña María prepara el desayuno:
café, leche, tostadas con mantequilla
y galletas.

Juan
Buenos días, amor mío.

doña María
Buenos días, cariño. Aquí tienes tu
café con leche y tu tostada. Y aquí
está el azúcar.

Juan
Gracias, pero no quiero tomar
azúcar. Estoy a régimen.

doña María
Muy bien, aquí está la sacarina.

Elena
Hola, mamá, yo sí quiero azúcar.
No estoy a régimen.

Elena
Mamá, yo quiero una taza de leche
caliente con galletas.

doña María
Ya son las ocho y media, y el auto-
bús sale a las nueve menos veinte.
¿Dónde está Dolores?

Juan
Todavía está en el cuarto de baño.

doña María
Pues, ya no puede desayunar.
Es muy tarde.

The narrator
Juan y los niños se marchan.
Doña María se queda sola en la casa.
Se sienta, se bebe su café con leche
y se come unas galletas.

and gets dressed. Elena also gets up.
Doña María prepares breakfast:
coffee, milk, toast with butter
and biscuits.

Good morning, my love.

Good morning, darling. Here is your
(white) coffee and your toast.
And here is the sugar.

Thank you, but I don't want any
sugar. I'm on a diet.

OK then, here are the sweeteners.

Hello Mummy. I want some sugar
though. I am not on a diet.

Mummy, I would like a cup of hot milk
with biscuits.

It is already half past eight and
the bus leaves at twenty to nine.
Where is Dolores?

She is still in the bathroom.

Then she can't have any breakfast.
It's too late.

Juan and the children set off. Doña
María remains alone in the house.
She sits down, drinks her (white)
coffee and eats a few biscuits.

EJERCICIOS

 Ejercicio 1:

¿Cuántos hijos tiene? – **How many children are there all together?**

E **Ejemplo – Example:**

Voz: *Tengo dos niñas y un niño.*
           I have two girls and one boy.

Usted: *Tiene tres hijos.*
           He/she has three children.

Voz: *Tiene tres hijos.*

Usted: *Tiene tres hijos.*

 Y ahora usted, por favor – and now you:

1. Tengo dos niñas y un niño.   I have two girls and one boy.
   Tiene tres hijos.   He/she has three children.

2. Tengo dos hijas. No tengo hijos.   I have two daughters. I don't have any sons.
   Tiene dos hijas.   He/she has two daughters.

3. Tengo dos hijos y tres hijas.   I have two sons and three daughters.
   Tiene cinco hijos.   .   He/she has four sons.

4. Tengo cuatro niños. No tengo niñas.   I have four boys. I don't have any girls.
   Tiene cuatro hijos.   He/she has four sons.

5. No tengo niños.   I don't have any children.
   No tiene hijos.   He/she doesn't have any children.

6. Tengo una niña y un niño.	I have a girl and a boy.
Tiene dos hijos.	He/she has two children.
7. Tengo cinco hijos y una hija.	I have five sons and one daughter.
Tiene seis hijos.	He/she has six children.

 Ejercicio 2:

Forme frases completas con el verbo *"levantarse"* – Form complete sentences using the verb *"levantarse"* (to get up).

E **Ejemplo – Example:**

Voz: **Doña María**

Usted: **Doña María se levanta.**
Doña María gets up.

Voz: **Doña María se levanta.**

Usted: **Doña María se levanta.**

 Y ahora usted, por favor – and now you:

1. Doña María
Doña María se levanta.   Doña María gets up.

2. Doña María y don Juan
Doña María y don Juan se levantan.   Doña María and Don Juan get up.

3. nosotros
Nos levantamos.   We get up.

4. tú
   Te levantas.   You get up.

5. ellos
   Se levantan.   They get up.

6. yo
   Me levanto.   I get up.

7. vosotros
   Os levantáis.   You get up.

Ejercicio 3:
Diga que lo hace – Say that he /she does it.

 Ejemplo – Example:

Voz: *Doña María quiere levantarse.*
Doña María wants to get up.

Usted: *Doña María quiere levantarse y se levanta.*
Doña María wants to get up and gets up.

Voz: *Doña María quiere levantarse
y se levanta.*

Usted: *Doña María quiere levantarse
y se levanta.*

Y ahora usted, por favor – and now you:

1. Doña María quiere levantarse.
   Doña María quiere levantarse
   y se levanta.

   Doña María wants to get up.
   Doña María wants to get up
   and gets up.

2. Juan quiere ducharse.
   Juan quiere ducharse y se ducha.

   Juan wants to shower and showers.

3. Dolores quiere prepararse.
   Dolores quiere prepararse
   y se prepara.

   Dolores wants to get ready
   and gets ready.

4. Miguel quiere afeitarse.
   Miguel quiere afeitarse y se afeita.

   Miguel wants to shave and shaves.

5. Elena quiere comerse unas galletas
   y se come unas galletas.

   Elena would like to eat a few biscuits,
   and he eats a few biscuits.

6. Yo quiero marcharme.
   Yo quiero marcharme y me marcho.

   I want to go and I go.

7. Tú quieres quedarte.
   Tú quieres quedarte y te quedas.

   You want to stay and you stay.

GRAMÁTICA

The Address

The address is given as follows in Spain:
1. The name of the person. The name is preceded by D. (don), for men, and by **Dª** (doña) for women. For childeren only the name is used. It is uncommon to use *señor, señora* or *señorita* as is often though by foreigners.
2. Postcode and town/city. Spanish postcodes consist of five digits, e.g. 28002 Madrid.
3. Street and house number. *Calle* is usually abbreviated with a c/. A comma is placed between the street name and the house number, e.g. *c/Sagasta, 11*
4. Floor and flat. When you give an address in Spain you don't only give the street and house number but also the floor and flat. The floor is given by the number of the floor following by a raised º, e.g. *2º (segundo)*. The various flats on a floor usually have a letter to distinguish them.

Example:
Doña María vive en Madrid, en la calle Sagasta, número ocho, segundo B.
Doña María lives in Madrid, at Sagasta Street, number 8, second floor, flat B.

Supplementary Exercise 1

Say where the following people live.

Example: D. Antonio Gil López, 46010 Valencia, c/Flora, 11, 3ºA; Don Antonio vive en Valencia, calle Flora, número once, tercero A.
1. D. Antonio Gil López, 46010 Valencia, c/Flora, 11, 3ºA.
2. Dª Ester Sánchez García, 14009 Córdoba, c/Creta, 39, 4ºC.
3. D. Esteban Pérez Martínez, 37008 Salamanca, c/Jardines, 14, 1ºB.
4. Dª Sofía Lozano Garrido, 45001 Toledo, c/Cuesta Alcázar, 22, 5ºB.

The Ordinal Numbers

The ordinal numbers from one to ten are:

primero/a	first
segundo/a	second
tercero/a	third
cuarto/a	fourth
quinto/a	fifth
sexto/a	sixth
séptimo/a	seventh
octavo/a	eight
noveno/a	ninth
décimo/a	tenth

The Verb „*ser*"

Spanish has two different verbs for „to be": *ser* and *estar*.

The verb *estar* indicates that something or someone is situated at a particular location:
(*Juan está en Málaga* - Juan is in Málaga) or that something is temporary (*Está cansado* – he is tired).
In contrast, the verb ser indicates that something is generally applicable or is always the case. (*Doña María es simpática.* - Doña María is nice. OR *Doña María es ama de casa.* - Doña María is a housewife.) It is also used to identify someone or something (*Éste es Alfonso* – this is Alfonso).

The difference between "generally applicable" and "temporary" becomes apparent from the way *está casado* (he is married) and *es soltero* (he is single) are used. *Es soltero* – describes a state in which every person naturally exists and in which they will remain unless they actively do something about it. If someone were to say *está soltero*, then he would be expressing the fact that he considers the state to be temporary (he is single at the moment). *Está casado* – describes a state, which if it happens at all, must first of all be established.

It is often difficult to explain the use of *ser* and *estar*. This is probably one of the main difficulties of Spanish. So be patient here.

The verb *ser* is conjugated irregularly

		SER (Present)
	1. Pers.	*soy*
Singular	2. Pers.	*eres*
	3. Pers.	*es*
	1. Pers.	*somos*
Plural	2. Pers.	*sois*
	3. Pers.	*son*

hijo – hija / hijos –hijas

el hijo	the son
la hija	the daughter

The plural form is masculine:
   los hijos – the sons OR the sons and the daughters, i.e. the children

The plural form is only feminine when you are only talking about daughters (and not sons):
   las hijas – the daughters

Example:
   Doña María tiene tres hijos.   Doña María has three children.

For *niño, niña* and *niños* the situation is identical:

el niño	the male child/boy
la niña	the female child/girl
los niños	the children
las niñas	the girls

Example:
   Doña María tiene tres hijos: dos niñas y un niño.
   Doña María has three children: two girls and a boy.

The Reflexive Verbs

se levanta	he/she gets up
se ducha	he/she showers
se arregla	he/she gets ready
se viste	he/she gets dressed

All four verbs are reflexive verbs. These are formed, as in other European languages, using the verb together with the reflexive pronoun – in Spanish *se*.

ducharse	to shower (oneself)

Example:
Doña María se levanta, se ducha, se arregla y se viste.
Doña María gets (herself) up, showers (herself), gets (herself) ready and dresses (herself).

The Reflexive Pronouns:

		DUCHARSE (Present)
	1. Pers.	*me ducho*
Singular	2. Pers.	*te duchas*
	3. Pers.	*se ducha*
	1. Pers.	*nos duchamos*
Plural	2. Pers.	*os ducháis*
	3. Pers.	*se duchan*

Examples:

Doña María se ducha.	Doña María showers.
Don Juan se ducha y los hijos se duchan.	Don Juan showers and the children shower.
Yo me ducho y tú te duchas.	I shower and you shower.
Nosotros nos duchamos y vosotros os ducháis.	We shower and they shower.

Other reflexive verbs:

se despierta	he/she wakes up
se afeita	he shaves
se maquilla	she puts on makeup
se marcha	he/she leaves
se queda	he/she stays
se sienta	he/she sits down
se bebe su café	he/she drinks his/her coffee
se come unas galleta	he/she eats a few biscuits

The verbs **beber** and **comer** which we have already met as non-reflexive verbs are used here in their reflexive form. The non-reflexive use of the verb indicates a situation which is more general. If a particular person eats or drinks something specific then the reflexive form is usually used:

Examples:

Juan se bebe un café.	Juan drinks a coffee.
Doña María se come unas galletas.	Doña María eats some biscuits.
Yo me tomo una cerveza.	I drink a beer.

The Verb *"sentarse"*

The verb **sentarse** (to sit down) changes its root vowel for all persons in the singular and for the third person plural:

SENTARSE (Present)		
Singular	1. Pers.	*me siento*
	2. Pers.	*te sientas*
	3. Pers.	*se sienta*
Plural	1. Pers.	*nos sentamos*
	2. Pers.	*os sentáis*
	3. Pers.	*se sientan*

Example:

Doña María se sienta.	Doña María sits down.

The Verb "vestirse"

The verb **vestirse** (to get dressed / to dress) belongs to the group of verbs ending in –_ir._ The conjugation deviates, in part, from the standard pattern. In the singular and the third person plural the root vowel changes

VESTIRSE (Present)		
Singular	1. Pers.	_me visto_
	2. Pers.	_te vistes_
	3. Pers.	_se viste_
Plural	1. Pers.	_nos vestimos_
	2. Pers.	_os vestís_
	3. Pers.	_se visten_

Examples:
 Doña María se viste. Don Juan se viste y los niños se visten.
 Yo me visto y tú te vistes.
 Nosotros nos vestimos y vosotros os vestís.

Conjugation of Verbs Ending in -_er_

Comer and **beber** are conjugated regularly and follow the pattern for the -_er_ conjugation:

CONJUGATION OF REGULAR VERBS ENDING IN -ER

COMER (Present)		
Singular	1. Pers.	_como_
	2. Pers.	_comes_
	3. Pers.	_come_
Plural	1. Pers.	_comemos_
	2. Pers.	_coméis_
	3. Pers.	_comen_

Summary of the Three Conjugations

The present forms of the verbs *tomar, comer* and *vivir*

		-AR	-ER	-IR
	1. Pers.	tomo	como	vivo
Singular	2. Pers.	tomas	comes	vives
	3. Pers.	toma	come	vive
	1. Pers.	tomamos	comemos	vivimos
Pluria	2. Pers.	tomáis	coméis	vivís
	3. Pers.	toman	comen	viven

Subject and Object of a Verb

Spanish nouns (and their articles) are not modified to denote that they are the subject or object of a verb.

*Éste es **el** café solo*	AND	*Prefiero **el** café con leche.*
el café (subject)		the coffee
el café (object)		the coffee
*Éste es **el** café solo*	AND	*Prefiero **el** café con leche.*
This is the black coffee	AND	I prefer the white coffee
(subject)		(object of to prefer)
la casa (subject)		the house
la casa (object)		the house
*Ésta es **la** casa de Carmen*	AND	*Prefiero **la** casa de María. –*
This is Carmen's house	AND	I prefer Maria's house
(subject)		(object)

If a person is being referred to, the preposition a is used to denote the object:

Examples:

Doña María despierta a Juan.	Doña María wakes Juan (object of to wake).
Doña María despierta a los niños.	Doña María wakes the children (object of to wake)

The verb *despertar* is conjugated using the same pattern as the verb *preferir,* i.e. the endings follow the regular *-ar* conjugation with the root vowel changing in the singular and the third person plural.

Example:

Doña María despierta a Juan, su marido.	Doña María wakes Juan her husband.

"Marido" – "mujer"

el hombre	the man
la mujer	the woman
el marido	the husband
la mujer	the wife

In formal situations, the expression *esposo* (meaning spouse) is used for the husband and *esposa* or *señora* for the wife. *Los esposos* means a married couple.

The Possessive Pronouns

POSSESSIVE PRONOUNS		
Singular	1. Pers.	mi
	2. Pers.	tu
	3. Pers.	su
Plural	1. Pers.	nuestro/a
	2. Pers.	vuestro/a
	3. Pers.	su

The possessive pronoun precedes the noun and is not modified.

The only exception is in the first and second person plural where a distinction must be made between the masculine and feminine form. The form agrees with the noun:

Examples:

nuestro hijo	our son
nuestra hija	our daughter
vuestro hijo	your son
vuestra hija	your daughter

The English forms *his* and *her* are both conveyed by the Spanish word **su**:
Examples:

Juan y *su hijo*   Juan and *his* son
María y *su hijo*.   María and *her* son

The possessive pronoun does not change in the third person
– irrespective of whether the noun is masculine or feminine:

– *Éste es su hijo y ésta es su hija.*   That is *his* son and that is *his* daughter.

– or whether one or more people are doing the possessing:

Éste es Juan, y Miguel es su hijo.   That is *Juan* and Miguel is *his* son.
Éstos son Juan y María,   That is *Juan* and *María*,
y Miguel es su hijo.   and Miguel is *their* son.

All possessive pronouns end with an *–s* if they refer to a noun in the plural:

yo	– *Estos niños son mis hijos.*
tú	– *Estos niños son tus hijos.*
él/ella/ usted	– *Estos niños son sus hijos.*
nosotros	– *Estos niños son nuestros hijos.*
vosotros	– *Estos niños son vuestros hijos.*
Ellos/ellas/ustedes	– *Estos niños son sus hijos.*

Caliente

The adjective **caliente** is not dependent on gender:

la leche caliente
la tostada caliente
el té caliente
el café caliente

If, however, the noun is in the plural then an *–s* is added:

las tostadas calientes

los cafés calientes

Information about the Country

The Spanish School System

In Spanish a distinction is made between *aprender* and *estudiar*.
The verb *aprender* is used to refer to learning in general, i.e. learning in the sense of increasing one's knowledge or ability to do something.
The verb *estudiar* is used to mean learning in the sense of intellectual learning such as learning or studying at school or university.
It is possible to say *Miguel, Dolores y Javier estudian*, although they go to completely different institutions:

Miguel estudia en la universidad.	Miguel is at university (lit: studies at the university).
Dolores estudia primero de bachillerato.	Dolores is at sixth-form college; in the first year (lit: studies first of sixth-form college).
Elena estudia segundo de educación primaria.	Elena is in the second year of primary school (lit: studies second of primary school).

Primary school is popularly known as *el colegio* or in its shortened from as *el cole*.
Carmen goes to school.   *Carmen va al colegio.*

School in general is called l*a escuela*.
The children go to school. – *Los niños van a la escuela.*

Estudiar does not only mean to learn or to study, but also "to go to school".

Elena estudia.	Elena goes to school.
Miguel estudia.	Miguel goes to university.

The Spanish school system is currently undergoing a process of reform.
It is structured as follows:

STRUCTURE OF SPANISH SCHOOL SYSTEM

In English there are no exact equivalents to the Spanish terms for
the individual tiers of the school system.
We have tried to convey the approximate meaning of these terms
in the following table.

0–6 years:	*Educación Infantil*	(pre-school, nursery school)
6–12 years:	*Educación Primaria*	(primary school [compulsory for everyone])
12–16 years:	*Educación Secundaria Obligatoria* abbreviation *E.S.O.*	(secondary school [compulsory for everyone])
16–18 years:	*Bachillerato*	(sixth-form or sixth-form college) or
	Formación Profesional	(technical college)
18 years and above:	*Universidad*	(university)

El bachillerato refers to the sixth-form college as an institution. If the building is
meant then *el instituto or el instituto de bachillerato*:
> *Dolores va al instituto a las ocho y media de la mañana.*
> Dolores goes to school at half past eight in the morning
> (sixth-form college).

La educación infantil refers to pre-school education. *La guardería* is the building
where the nursery school or "Kindergarden" is located.

Examples:

Miguel tiene 19 años. Estudia en la universidad.	Miguel is 19 and goes to university.
Dolores tiene 17 años y estudia primero de bachillerato.	Dolores ist 17 and is in the first year of the sixth-form college.
Elena tiene 8 años y estudia educación primaria.	Elena is 8 and is at primary school.

Meals of the Day

Many Spaniards only eat a few biscuits *(galletas)* for breakfast or drink a coffee or a glass of milk. The reason for this is that the evening meal is usually very filling and is eaten relatively late, between 8 p.m. and 10 p.m. A second breakfast is taken between 11 a.m. and midday – usually coffee and toast or **churros**. Lunch is taken between 2 p.m. and 4 p.m.. The restaurants are open during this period. At around 6 p.m. coffee is drunk again with a piece of cake, some biscuits or an open sandwich.

The Family

el abuelo y la abuela
(los abuelos)

el padre + la madre (los padres)

el hijo y la hija (los hijos)

el nieto y la nieta (los nietos)

el abuelo y la abuela
(los abuelos)

Spanish does not have an equivalent to the terms *parents* or *grandparents*. If the father and the mother or the grandfather and the grandmother are meant then the masculine forms are simply used in the plural. You say *los padres* (literally, the fathers) and *los abuelos* (literally, the grandfathers). *Los hijos* and *los nietos* behave in the same way.

Supplementary Exercise 2

We will look at family relationships in the following exercise. A number of terms will be used which you have not yet learnt. But from the context you will be able to easily work out their meaning:

Doña María tiene tres hijos, Miguel, Dolores y Elena. Doña María es la madre de Miguel, Dolores y Elena, y don José es el padre. Doña María y don José son los padres. La madre de doña María es la abuela de los niños y la madre de don José también. El padre de doña María es el abuelo de los niños, igual que el padre de don José. Los padres de doña María y don José son los abuelos de los niños y éstos son los nietos de sus abuelos. Dolores es la hermana de Miguel y Elena. Miguel es el hermano de Dolores y Elena. Miguel, Dolores y Elena son hermanos.

Supplementary Exercise 3
Answer the following questions regarding relationships in Doña María's family.

Example: ¿Qué relación tiene doña María con don José? Doña María es la mujer de don José.
1. ¿Qué relación tiene doña María con don José?
2. ¿Qué relación tiene Elena con Dolores?
3. ¿Qué relación tiene don José con Miguel?
4. ¿Qué relación tienen Miguel, Dolores y Elena con doña María y don José?

Solutions to the Supplementary Exercises

Supplementary Exercise 1

1. Don Antonio vive en Valencia, calle Flora, número once, tercero A.
2. Doña Ester vive en Bilbao, calle Creta, número treinta y nueve, cuarto C.
3. Don Esteban vive en Salamanca, calle Jardines, número catorce, primero B.
4. Doña Sofía vive en Toledo, calle Cuesta Alcázar, número veintidós, quinto B.

Supplementary Exercise 2

Doña María has three children, Miguel, Dolores and Elena. Doña María is the mother of Miguel, Dolores und Elena, and Don José is the father. Doña María and Don José are the parents. The mother of Doña María is the grandmother of the children, and so is the mother of Don José. The father of Doña María is the grandfather of the children, just like the father of Don José. The parents of Doña María and Don José are the grandparents of the children and they are the grandchildren of their grandparents. Dolores is the sister of Miguel and Elena. Miguel is the brother of Dolores and Elena. Miguel, Dolores and Elena are brothers and sisters (siblings).

Supplementary Exercise 3

1. Doña María es la mujer de don José.
2. Elena es la hermana de Dolores.
3. Don José es el padre de Miguel.
4. Miguel, Dolores y Elena son los hijos de doña María y don José.

LECCIÓN 7

Doña María va de compras

In this lesson you will learn how to talk about the following subjects:
- the family
- personal hygiene
- school
- the bank
- the department store

CD2
TOP14 Remember the following phrases:

Quiero sacar treinta mil pesetas de mi cuenta corriente.	I would like to withdraw 30,000 pesetas from my current account
Rellene este formulario.	Fill out this form.
Escriba su número de cuenta.	Enter (write) your account number.
Aquí tiene.	There you are (lit: Here you have).
¿Cómo quiere el dinero?	How do you want the money?
cambiar marcos en pesetas	to exchange pounds for pesetas
cambiar un billete de cinco mil en cinco billetes de mil peseta notes	to change a five thousand peseta note into five one thousand
pagar con tarjeta	to pay by credit card
pagar en efectivo	to pay in cash
sacar dinero del cajero automático	to withdraw money from a cash dispenser
pagar con un cheque	to pay by cheque
Hoy es viernes.	Today is Friday.
los días de la semana:	the days of the week
lunes	Monday
martes	Tuesday
miércoles	Wednesday
jueves	Thursday
viernes	Friday
sábado	Saterday
domingo	Sunday

¿Desea algo más?	Is there anything else?
¿Cuánto es?	How much does it cost?/ How much must I pay?
el siguiente, por favor	the next, please
unos pantalones de verano	a pair of summer trousers
si es posible de algodón	if possible, in cotton
Busco algo más cómodo.	I am looking for something more comfortable.
Están muy bien de precio.	It is very reasonable.
Pruébese algunos.	Try it on.
¿Dónde están los probadores?	Where are the changing cubicles?
las estaciones del año:	the seasons
la primavera	spring
el verano	summer
el otoño	autumn
el invierno	winter
Los colores:	the colours
blanco	white
negro	black
rojo	red
azul	blue
verde	green
amarillo	yellow
marrón	brown
gris	grey
de color claro	light
de color oscuro	dark
de colores	colourful / brightly-coloured

A: DIÁLOGOS

CD2 **The story:**
TOP 13 On Friday Doña María has more things than usual to do. She has to do some shopping in the department store and go to the post office. First of all though she goes to the bank to get the money she will need.

Narrator
Hoy es viernes y doña María va a la ciudad. Primero va al banco.

Today is Friday and Doña María is going into the town. First of all she goes to the bank.

María
Buenos días.

Good day.

Bank clerk
Buenos días, señora. ¿Qué desea?

Good day. What can I do for you (what do you desire)?

María
Quiero sacar treinta mil pesetas de mi cuenta corriente.

I would like to withdraw thirty thousand pesetas from my current account.

Bank clerk
Muy bien, rellene este impreso, por favor. Escriba su número de cuenta y la cantidad de dinero que quiere sacar.

OK, fill out this form, please. Enter your account number and the amount you wish to withdraw.

María
Aquí tiene.

There you are.

Bank clerk
Muy bien. ¿Cómo quiere el dinero, en billetes de diez mil, de cinco mil o en billetes de mil pesetas?

Good. How would you like the money: in ten thousand, five thousand or one thousand peseta notes?

María
Cuatro billetes de cinco mil y diez billetes de mil, por favor.

Four five thousands and ten one thousand please.

Bank clerk
Aquí tiene, treinta mil pesetas.

Here you are, thirty thousand pesetas.

María
Muchas gracias, adiós.   Many thanks, goodbye.

Bank clerk
Adiós, señora y buenos días.   Goodbye madam, have a pleasant day.

The story:
Doña María goes to the post office because she needs some stamps and wants to pick up a parcel:

María
Buenos días.   Good day.

Post office clerk
Buenos días. ¿Qué desea?   What can I do for you?

María
Deme dos sellos de treinta y cinco   Please give me two 35 peseta stamps
pesetas, por favor y un sello de setenta. and one 70 peseta stamp.

Post office clerk
Aquí tiene. ¿Desea algo más?   Here you are. Would you like
                                          anything else?

María
Sí, quiero recoger un paquete.   Yes, I would like to pick up a parcel.
Aquí tiene el resguardo.   Here's the (lit: have/take) the delivery
                                          notification.

Post office clerk
Un momento, por favor. ... Aquí está   One moment please. ... Here's the
el paquete. Doña María Fernández   parcel. Doña María Fernández García,
García, calle Sagasta, número ocho,   Sagasta Street, number 8, second floor,
segundo B.   flat B.

María
Muchas gracias. ¿Cuánto es?   Thank you. How much do I owe you?

Post office clerk
Dos sellos de treinta y cinco, y uno   Two stamps at 35 pesetas and one at
de setenta, son ciento cuarenta pesetas. 70 pesetas; that's 140 pesetas.

María
Aquí tiene, ciento cuarenta pesetas.   There you are, 140 pesetas.

Post office clerk
Correcto.   Correct.

María
Adiós.   Goodbye.

Post office clerk
Adiós. El siguiente, por favor.   Goodbye. The next please.

The story:
Doña María needs a new pair of trousers. So, first of all, she goes to the department store. The most famous chain of department stores in Spain is EL CORTE INGLÉS. To orientate herself she first of all listens to the announcement.

Announcement
Bienvenidos al CORTE INGLÉS. Welcome to Corte Inglés.
En la planta sótano se encuentra In the basement is our
nuestro supermercado con las supermarket with fish, meat,
secciones de pescado, de carne, fruit and vegetable departments.
y de fruta y verdura. En la planta On the ground floor you
baja tienen la sección de perfumería will find our perfume and
y cosmética, la sección de discos, cosmetics department, the record
la librería y la papelería. En la pri- department and the book and
mera planta se encuentra toda la stationery departments. On the first
moda de señoras, chicos, niños y floor is ladies and childrens wear. On
bebés. En la segunda planta la moda the second floor menswear, the
de caballeros, la sección de electrical department, computer
electrónica, la de informática y la department and the hairdresser's. On
peluquería. En la tercera planta se the third floor is the sports
encuentra la sección de deporte department and our cafeteria.
y nuestra cafetería.

The story:
in the fruit and vegetable department.

Announcement
Nuestras ofertas de frutería: Offers in our fruit and vegetable
                                         department:
plátanos kilo 200 pesetas   bananas 200 pesetas/kg
manzanas kilo 220 pesetas   apples 220 pesetas/kg
naranjas kilo 150 pesetas   oranges 150 pesetas/kg
mandarinas kilo 210 pesetas   mandarins 210 pesetas/kg
uvas kilo 240 pesetas   grapes 240 pesetas/kg
peras kilo 230 pesetas   pears 230 pesetas/kg

fresas kilo 420 pesetas	strawberries 200 pesetas/kg
patatas 5 kilos 250 pesetas	potatoes 5 kg 250 pesetas
lechuga pieza 70 pesetas	lettuce 70 pesetas each
zanahorias bolsa 140 pesetas	carrots 140 peseta per bag
pimientos verdes kilo 440 pesetas	green peppers 440 pesetas/kg
pimientos rojos kilo 220 pesetas	red peppers 440 pesetas/kg
tomates kilo 250 pesetas.	tomatoes 250 pesetas/kg.

The story:
Doña María wants to buy herself a pair of trousers.

Narrator

Doña María quiere comprar unos pantalones. Por eso sube a la primera planta, a la sección de señoras.

Doña María would like to buy a pair of trousers. So she goes to the first floor to the ladieswear department.

Saleslady

¿Qué desea?

What would you like?

María

Quiero unos pantalones de verano, de color claro, talla cuarenta y dos, y si es posible de algodón.

I am looking for (would like) a pair of summer trousers, in a light colour, size 42 and, if possible, in cotton.

Saleslady

Aquí tenemos unos pantalones muy elegantes.

We have a very elegant pair (of trousers) here.

María

No no, yo busco algo más cómodo y más económico.

No, no, I am looking for something more comfortable and more reasonable.

Saleslady

¿Y estos pantalones?, están muy bien de precio. Son de algodón y son comodísimos. Y el color es muy alegre. ¡Pruébese algunos!

And (what about) this pair here? They are very good value. They are in cotton and very comfortable. And the colour is very appealing. Try it on.

María

Muy bien, ¿dónde están los probadores?

OK then, where are the changing cubicles?

Saleslady
Vaya todo recto y al final, a la derecha
están los probadores de señora.

Go straight ahead. At the end on the
right are the ladies' changing cubicles.

María
Muchas gracias.

Many thanks.

EJERCICIOS

Ejercicio 1:

CD2
TOP14
Diga que quiere hacer lo mismo – Say that you want to do the same thing.

E Ejemplo – Example:

Voz: *Un señor cambia euros en pesetas.*
A man exchanges euros for pesetas.

Usted: *Quiero cambiar euros en pesetas.*
I want to exchange euros for pesetas.

Voz: *Quiero cambiar euros en pesetas.*

Usted: *Quiero cambiar euros en pesetas.*

Y ahora usted, por favor – and now you:

1. Un señor cambia euros en pesetas.
   Quiero cambiar euros en pesetas.　　I want to exchange euros for pesetas.

2. Otro señor cambia pesetas en euros.
   Quiero cambiar pesetas en euros.　　I want to exchange pesetas for euros.

3. Una señora paga con tarjeta.
   Quiero pagar con tarjeta.　　I would like to pay by creditcard.

4. Otra señora paga en efectivo.
   Quiero pagar en efectivo.　　I would like to pay in cash.

5. Un señor saca dinero del cajero automático.
   Quiero sacar dinero del cajero automático.　　I would like to withdraw some money from the cash dispenser.

6. Otro señor paga con un cheque.
   Quiero pagar con un cheque.　　I would like to pay by cheque.

7. Otro señor cambia un billete de cinco mil pesetas en cinco billetes de mil.
   Quiero cambiar un billete de cinco mil pesetas en cinco billetes de mil.　　I would like to change one five thousand peseta note for five one thousand peseta notes.

Ejercicio 2:

Diga que lo haga – Use the imperative

E Ejemplo – Example:

Voz: *Lucía no quiere bailar.*
Lucía doesn't want to dance.

Usted: *Lucía, baila, por favor.*
Lucía, dance please.

Voz: *Lucía, baila, por favor.*

Usted: *Lucía, baila, por favor.*

Y ahora usted, por favor – and now you:

1. Lucía no quiere bailar.
   Lucía, baila, por favor.

   Lucía doesn't want to dance.
   Lucía, dance please.

2. Antonio no quiere estudiar.
   Antonio, estudia, por favor.

   Antonio, study (do your
   homework) please.

3. Jorge no quiere pagar la cuenta.
   Jorge, paga la cuenta, por favor.

   Jorge, pay the bill please.

4. Carmen no quiere salir.
   Carmen, sal, por favor.

   Carmen, go (come) out please

5. Carlos no quiere venir.
   Carlos, ven, por favor.

   Carlos, come please.

6. Rosa no quiere comer.
   Rosa, come, por favor.

   Rosa, eat please.

7. Rosana no quiere despertarse.
   Rosana, despiértate, por favor.

   Rosana, wake up please.

Ejercicio 3:
Diga donde lo puede comprar – Say where you can buy these things.

 Ejemplo – Example:

Voz: *¿Dónde puedo comprar fruta?*
         Where can I buy fruit?

Usted: *En la frutería.*
         In the fruit shop

Voz: *En la frutería.*

Usted: *En la frutería.*

 Y ahora usted, por favor – and now you:

1. ¿Dónde puedo comprar fruta?   Where can I buy fruit?
   En la frutería.   In the fruit shop.

2. ¿Dónde puedo comprar pescado?   Where can I buy fish.
   En la pescadería.   At the fishmonger's.

3. ¿Dónde puedo comprar libros?   Where can I buy books?
   En la librería.   In the bookshop.

4. ¿Dónde puedo comprar carne?   Where can I buy meat?
   En la carnicería.   At the butcher's.

5. ¿Dónde puedo comprar pan?   Where can I buy bread?
   En la panadería.   At the baker's.

6. ¿Dónde puedo tomar café?   Where can I drink coffee?
   En la cafetería.   In the cafeteria.

7. ¿Dónde puedo arreglarme el pelo?   Where can I have my hair done?
   En la peluquería.   At the hairdresser's.

GRAMÁTICA

The Imperative

Usually the imperative form is used to tell someone to do something. When forming the imperative in Spanish, a distinction must be made between the second person *(tú)* and the polite form *(usted)* as well as between the singular and the plural. In addition to this, there are three different types of verb: verbs ending in *–ar, –er* and *–ir*.

Imperative Forms for Verbs Ending in *-ar:*

	TOMAR (prendre)		
2nd person singular	(tú):	toma	(take)
2nd person plural	(vosotros):	tomad	(take)
polite form singular	(usted):	tome	(take)
polite form plural	(ustedes):	tomen	(take)

For verbs ending in *–ar,* the final *–r* is omitted from the infinitive for the second person singular:

llamar	⇒	llama	(call)
bailar	⇒	baila	(dance)
cantar	⇒	canta	(sing)
cenar	⇒	cena	(eat dinner)
desayunar	⇒	desayuna	(eat breakfast)

For the polite form the *–a-* becomes an *–e*:

tomar	⇒	tome	(take)
llamar	⇒	llame	(call)
bailar	⇒	baile	(dance)
cantar	⇒	cante	(sing)
cenar	⇒	cene	(eat dinner)
desayunar	⇒	desayune	(eat breakfast)

Imperative Forms for Verbs Ending in *-er.*

COMER (eat)			
2nd person singular	(tú):	come	(eat)
2nd person plural	(vosotros):	comed	(eat)
polite form singular	(usted):	coma	(eat)
polite form plural	(ustedes):	coman	(eat)

Again, for verbs ending in *–er*, the final *–r* is omitted from the infinitive for the second person singular:

comer	$\Rightarrow$	come	(eat)
beber	$\Rightarrow$	bebe	(drink)

For the polite from the *–e-* becomes an *–a*:

comer	$\Rightarrow$	coma	(eat)
beber	$\Rightarrow$	beba	(drink

Examples:

Anda, Carmen, come y bebe, por favor.	Come on, Carmen, eat and drink please.
Don Fernando, coma y beba, por favor.	Don Fernando, eat and drink please.

Imperative Forms for Verbs Ending in –*ir*:

VIVIR (to live)

2nd person singular	(tú):	vi**ve**	(live)
2nd person plural	(vosotros):	vi**vid**	(live)
polite form singular	(usted):	vi**va**	(live)
polite form plural	(ustedes):	vi**van**	(live)

Yet again, for verbs ending in –*ir*, the final –*r* is omitted from the infinitive for the second person singular, and the –*i* is replaced by an –*e*, exactly as for verbs ending in –*er*:

vi**vir**	⇒	vi**ve**	(live)
escri**bir**	⇒	escri**be**	(write)

For the polite form the –*i* replaced by an –*a:*

vi**vir**	⇒	vi**va**	(live)
escri**bir**	⇒	escri**ba**	(write)

The second person plural for all three types of verb is formed by replacing the –*r* of the infinitive with a –*d*:

tom**ar**	⇒	tom**ad**	(take)
com**er**	⇒	com**ed**	(eat)
vi**vir**	⇒	vi**vid**	(live)

The plural of the polite forms is formed by adding an –*n* to the singular of the polite form:

tom**e**	⇒	tom**en**	(take)
com**a**	⇒	com**an**	(eat)
vi**va**	⇒	vi**van**	(live)

Imperative forms of irregular verbs are also irregular:

SALIR (to go out / come out)

sal, Carmen	(go out/ come out, Carmen)
salid, niños	(go out/ come out, children)
salga, señor	(go out/ come out, Sir)
salgan, señores	(go out/ come out, gentlemen)

HACER (to do)

haz, Carmen	(do (it), Carmen)
haced, niños	(do (it), children)
haga, señor	(do (it), Sir)
hagan, señores	(do (it), gentlemen)

TENER (to have)

tten, Carmen	(have (it) , Carmen)
tened, niños	(have (it), children)
tenga, señor	(have (it), Sir)
tengan, señores	(have (it), gentlemen)

IR (to go)

ve, Carmen	(go, Carmen)
id, niños	(go, children)
vaya, señor	(go, Sir)
vayan, señores	(go, gentlemen)

VENIR (to come)

en, Carmen	(come, Carmen)
venid, niños	(come, children)
venga, señor	(come, Sir)
vengan, señores	(come, gentlemen)

Caution, do not confuse:

ve	go
ven	come

Supplementary Exercise 1

Read out loud.

Doña María tells her children what to do:

Miguel, despiértate. Son las siete y media, levántate y dúchate.
Dolores, por favor, ven a desayunar. Tómate un café y cómete unas galletas.
Javier, vístete y ven a la cocina. Anda, desayuna rápido, bébete la leche y cómete
la tostada.

For reflexive verbs the reflexive pronoun comes after the imperative form:

¡despiértate!	wake up!
¡levántate!	get up!
¡dúchate!	shower!
¡vístete!	get dressed!

Nouns Ending in "*-ería*"

A lot of words were used in the department store announcement which end
in *–ería:*

perfumería	perfumery
librería	book department / bookshop
papelería	stationery department / shop
peluquería	hairdresser
cafetería	cafeteria

All of these words refer to the location where the item contained in the root of the
word is manufactured, processed or sold:

el perfume (perfume)	⇒	*la perfumería*
el libro (book)	⇒	*la librería*
el papel (paper/stationery)	⇒	*la papelería*
la peluca (literally: wig)	⇒	*la peluquería*
		(hairdresser)
el café (coffee)	⇒	*la cafetería*

Example:

¿Dónde puedo comprar perfume?	Where can I buy perfume?
En la perfumería.	In the perfumery.

Other nouns ending in "*ería*":

carnicería	butcher's (shop)
panadería	baker's (shop)

cervecería	pub / brewery
frutería	greengrocer's (shop)
pescadería	fishmonger's (shop)

Supplementary Exercise 2

Read the following short dialogues which take place at the information desk at Corte Inglés:

– *Quiero comprar plátanos.*
– *Vaya a la frutería. Está en la planta sótano.*

– *Dónde está la peluquería?*
– *Se encuentra en la tercera planta.*

– *Quiero comprar un perfume.*
– *Vaya a la perfumería. Está en la planta baja.*

Now give the appropriate answer.
Example: Quiero comprar fruta. – Vaya a la frutería. Está en la planta sótano.
1. Quiero comprar fruta.
2. Quiero comprar un perfume.
3. Quiero comprar una guía turística.
4. Quiero comprar cerveza.

Asking how much something costs or asking for the bill

 Instead of saying ¿*Cuánto es?* (literally: how much is it?) you can also say ¿*Cuánto cuesta?* (How much does it cost?) or ¿*Qué le debo?* (What do I owe you? / What shall I give you?). In a bar or restaurant people often just say *La cuenta, por favor* (the bill, please).

Examples:
Un sello para Alemania, por favor.
Aquí tiene.
¿Cuánto es?
Sesenta y cinco pesetas, por favor.

Camarero, la cuenta, por favor.
Aquí tiene, son tres mil doscientas cincuenta pesetas.

¿Cuánto cuesta una habitación individual una noche?
Seis mil quinientas pesetas.

 **By the way:** A recent development is that, when paying in cash, prices are rounded up or down avoiding the need for small denomination peseta coins.

Clothing

Articles of clothing which you should know:

la camisa	shirt
la chaqueta	jacket
el vestido	dress
el jersey	pullover
los calcetines	socks / stockings
el bañador	bathing trunks or bathing costume
los zapatos	shoes
los pantalones	trousers
los vaqueros	jeans

Pantalones (trousers) take the plural form even if only one pair of trousers is meant.

Example:

Doña María quiere comprarse unos pantalones.	Doña María would like to buy some trousers.

Accordingly, the adjective agrees with the plural form for pantalones:

Tengo unos pantalones elegantes.	I have an elegant pair of trousers.

Los vaqueros (jeans) also takes the plural form.

Example:

Me gustan tus vaqueros.	I like your jeans.
Quiero unos vaqueros blancos.	I am looking for a pair of white jeans.

141

The most important colours

blanco	white
negro	black
rojo	red
azul	blue
verde	green
amarillo	yellow
marrón	brown
gris	grey
de colores	brightly-coloured
de color claro	light
de color oscuro	dark

Some Verbs which Indicate Motion

Subir means "to move in an upward direction", this can be by foot, by lift, escalator or any other mode of transport.

Example:

Doña María sube a la primera planta. a) Doña María takes the lift up to the first floor. (in the department store);
b) Doña María goes up to the first floor.

In Spanish the mode of transport is not important. What is important though, is the direction of travel. Accordingly *subir* is used to mean "to go up" and *bajar* means "to go down" whilst ir or irse is used to mean "to leave or to go somewhere".

Examples:

Bajo al sótano.	I go down to the basement.
Subo a la primera planta.	I go up to the first floor.
Voy a Málaga.	I go to Málaga.

Supplementary Exercise 3

Translate:
1. I go to Málaga.
2. I go home.
3. I go down to the cellar.
4. I go up to the eighth floor.

Information about the country

Stamps

As well as at the post office, stamps can also be bought in Spain at the so-called ESTANCOS. These are state-run shops which primarily sell tobacco products. These shops can be recognized by the following symbol:

LOGOTIPO ESTANCO

A few points about food

Plátano is the word used for the bananas which are grown in the Canary Islands. They are smaller and have a stronger smell and flavour than bananas which come from Latin America. They are normally more expensive. The larger bananas which we know are also called *banana*.

In Spanish a distinction is made between *lechuga* and *ensalada*. *Lechuga* means lettuce in its unprocessed form, as bought in a shop. *Ensalada* on the other hand is a salad which is ready to eat. This can be a green salad, potato salad or any other sort of salad.

Some other foods which you should definitely know:

la sal	salt
la pimienta	pepper
la mermelada	jam / marmelade
el yogur	yoghurt
el pan	bread

Caution: la pimienta means pepper, whilst el pimiento means the vegetable pepper (green or red).

Bread is baked freshly every day in Spain. It usually comes in the form of a baguette type of bread. In recent years most bakers have been selling whole-meal bread. This type of bread doesn't usually keep long. Whole-meal bread is known as *pan integral*.

Supplementary Exercise 4

Read out what these people want to buy:
mujer:
Quiero un vestido de invierno, de color oscuro, talla treinta y ocho, y si es posible de lana. – I want (am looking for) a dark winter dress, size 39 and, if possible, in wool.

hombre:
Quiero unos zapatos negros de invierno, talla cuarenta y cuatro, y si es posible de piel. – I am looking for black winter shoes, size 44 and, if possible, in leather.

joven:
Quiero unos vaqueros blancos, talla veintiocho. – I am looking for a pair of white jeans, size 28.

Translate into Spanish:
Example: I would like a red jacket, size 40. – Quiero una chaqueta roja, talla cuarenta.
1. I would like a red jacket, size 40.
2. I would like some light summer shoes.
3. I would like a colourful summer shirt.
4. I would like a blue dress, size 46.

Solutions to the Supplementary Exercises

Supplementary Exercise 1
Miguel, wake up. It is half past seven, get up and shower. Dolores please come and have breakfast. Drink a coffee and eat some biscuits.
Elena, get dressed and come into the kitchen. Come on, hurry up (eat your breakfast quickly), drink the milk and eat the toast.

Supplementary Exercise 2

1. Vaya a la frutería. Está en la planta sótano.
2. Vaya a la perfumería. Está en la planta baja.
3. Vaya a la librería. Está en la planta baja.
4. Vaya al supermercado. Está en la planta sótano.

Supplementary Exercise 3

1. Voy a Málaga.
2. Voy a casa.
3. Bajo al sótano.
4. Subo a la octava planta.

Supplementary Exercise 4

1. Quiero una chaqueta roja, talla cuarenta.
2. Quiero unos zapatos de verano, de color claro.
3. Quiero una camisa de verano de colores.
4. Quiero un vestido azul, talla cuarenta y seis.

LECCIÓN 8

In this lesson you will learn how to:

– describe physical aliments

Remember the following expressions and phrases:

¿Qué pasa?	What's wrong?
¿Qué le pasa?	What's wrong with you?
¿Qué le pasa al niño?	What's wrong with the child?
¿Qué puedo hacer por usted?	What can I do for you?
Me duele mucho.	It is hurting me a lot.
Me duele mucho la cabeza.	I have a bad headache.
¿Tiene algún problema?	Do you have any problems?
Vamos a ver.	Let's have a look.
Enséñeme la mano.	Show me your hand.
Vaya usted al dentista.	Go to the dentist.
Woman: Estoy mala.	I am ill.
Man: Estoy malo.	I am ill.
Woman: Estoy enferma.	I am ill.
Man: Estoy enfermo.	I am ill.

148

CD2 DIÁLOGOS
TOP 18

The story: En el médico – at the doctor's.

Doctor
Buenos días, señorita, ¿qué le pasa?

Good day, Señorita, what is wrong with you?

Ana
Me duele mucho esta mano.

This hand is hurting me a lot.

Doctor
¿Se ha dado algún golpe?

Have you knocked yourself somehow?

Ana
Sí, jugando al baloncesto me he doblado la mano.

Yes while playing basketball, I twisted my hand.

Doctor
Vamos a ver. Enséñeme la mano.

Let's have a look. Show me your hand.

Doctor
Buenas tardes, señor, qué le pasa?

Good day, Señor, what's wrong with you?

Señor
Me duele mucho esta pierna.

This leg is hurting me a lot.

Doctor
¿Se ha dado algún golpe?

Have you knocked yourself somehow?

Señor
Sí, corriendo en bicicleta me he dado un golpe.

Yes, whilst cycling I knocked myself.

Doctor
Vamos a ver. Enséñeme la pierna.

Show me the leg.

Doctor
Buenas tardes, señorita, ¿qué le pasa?

Good day, Señorita, what's wrong with you?

Señorita
Me duele muchísimo la barriga.

I have terrible pains in the stomach.

Doctor
¿Ha comido algo especial?

Have you eaten anything in particular?

149

Señorita
He comido dos tabletas de chocolate y una caja de galletas.

I have eaten two bars of chocolate and a packet of biscuits.

Doctor
Pues no coma nada más en todo el día y beba mucha agua.

Then don't eat anything more today and drink lots of water.

Doctor
Buenos días, señor, ¿qué le pasa?

Good day, Señor, what's wrong with you?

Señor
Me duele mucho la cabeza.

I have a bad headache.

Doctor
¿Tiene algún problema?

Do you have any problems?

Señor
No, no tengo ningún problema, pero he estado bebiendo toda la noche.

No, but I spent the entire night drinking.

Doctor
Pues, vaya a casa a dormir y no beba más.

Then go home, sleep and don't drink anything else.

The scene:
In the following dialogues the doctor tells his patients to visit the appropriate specialist.

Doctor
¿Qué le pasa, señora?

What's wrong with you?

Señora
Me duele mucho una muela.

I have bad toothache.

Doctor
Vaya usted al dentista.

Go to the dentist.

Doctor
¿Qué le pasa al niño?

What's wrong with the boy/child?

Señora
Está enfermo. Tiene mucha fiebre.

He/she is ill. He/she has a high fever.

Doctor
Vayan ustedes al pediatra con el niño.

Go with (take) the child to the paediatrician.

Doctor
Buenos días, señora, ¿qué puedo hacer por usted?

Good day, what can I do for you?

Señora
Creo que estoy embarazada.

I think that I am pregnant.

Doctor
Entonces, vaya usted mejor al ginecólogo.

Then you'd better go to the gynaecologist.

EJERCICIOS

 Ejercicio 1:

Diga lo que le duele. – Say that the part of the body mentioned by the speaker is hurting you.

(E) Ejemplo – Example:

Voz:	*la mano*
	the hand
Usted:	*Me duele la mano.*
	My hand hurts.
Voz:	*Me duele la mano.*
Usted:	*Me duele la mano.*

 Y ahora usted, por favor – and now you:

1. la mano
   Me duele la mano.

2. la cabeza
   Me duele la cabeza.

3. la barriga
   Me duele la barriga.

4. las piernas
   Me duelen las piernas.

5. la garganta
   Me duele la garganta.

6. los pies
   Me duelen los pies.

7. los brazos
   Me duelen los brazos.

the hand
My hand hurts.

the head
I have a headache.

the stomach
I have stomach ache.

las piernas
My legs are hurting me.

the throat
I have a sore throat.

the feet
My feet are hurting me.

the arms
My arms are hurting me.

Ejercicio 2:

Ponga las frases en pretérito perfecto. – Repeat the following sentences but in the perfect.

E Ejemplo – Example:

Voz: *Visito la ciudad de Barcelona.*
I visit the city of Barcelona.

Usted: *He visitado la ciudad de Barcelona.*
I have visited the city of Barcelona.

Voz: *He visitado la ciudad de Barcelona.*

Usted: *He visitado la ciudad de Barcelona.*

 Y ahora usted, por favor – and now you:

1. Visito la ciudad de Barcelona. I visit the city of Barcelona.
   He visitado la ciudad de Barcelona. I have visited the city of Barcelona.

2. Me tomo una cerveza. I drink a beer.
   Me he tomado una cerveza. I have drunk a beer.

3. Compro unos pantalones en el I buy a pair of trousers at
   Corte Inglés. Corte Inglés.
   He comprado unos pantalones en I have bought a pair of trousers at
   el Corte Inglés. Corte Inglés.

4. Escribo una carta.
   He escrito una carta.

   I write a letter.
   I have written a letter.

5. Veo a Cati.
   He visto a Cati.

   I see Cati.
   I have seen Cati.

6. Pago la cuenta.
   He pagado la cuenta.

   I pay the bill.
   I have paid the bill.

7. Hablo con Carlos.
   He hablado con Carlos.

   I pay the bill.
   I have paid the bill.

Ejercicio 3:

Pregunte qué han hecho. – Ask what the people mentioned have done.

E Ejemplo – Example:

Voz: *tú*

Usted: *¿Qué has hecho?*
What have you done?

Voz: *¿Qué has hecho?*

Usted: *¿Qué has hecho?*

 Y ahora usted, por favor – and now you:

1. tú
   ¿Qué has hecho?   What have you done?

2. María
   ¿Qué ha hecho?   What has she done?

3. nosotros
   ¿Qué hemos hecho?   What has she done?

4. Luis y José
   ¿Qué han hecho?   What have they done?

5. yo
   ¿Qué he hecho?   What have I done?

6. usted
   ¿Qué ha hecho?   What have they done?

7. vosotros
   ¿Qué habéis hecho?   What have you done?

Ejercicio 4:
Diga que lo está haciendo – Say that you are doing the thing mentioned.

E **Ejemplo – Example:**

Voz: *¿Has firmado el cheque?*
Have you signed the cheque?

Usted: *Estoy firmando el cheque.*
I am signing the cheque (at the moment)

Voz: *Estoy firmando el cheque.*

Usted: *Estoy firmando el cheque.*

 Y ahora usted, por favor – and now you:

1. ¿Has firmado el cheque?
   Estoy firmando el cheque.

   Have you signed the cheque?
   I am signing the cheque
   (at the moment).

2. ¿Has comido un bocadillo?
   Estoy comiendo un bocadillo.

   Have you eaten a filled roll?
   I am eating a filled roll.

3. ¿Has leído el libro?
   Estoy leyendo el libro.

   Have you read the book?
   I am reading the book.

4. ¿Has vivido en Bilbao?
   Estoy viviendo en Bilbao.

   Have you lived in Bilbao?
   I am living in Bilbao (at the moment).

5. ¿Has escrito la carta a Miguel?
   Estoy escribiendo la carta a Miguel.

   Have you written the letter to Miguel?
   I am writing the letter to Miguel.

6. ¿Has comprado fruta?
   Estoy comprando fruta.

Have you bought any fruit?
I am buying some fruit.

7. Has visto a Luisa?
   Estoy viendo a Luisa.

Have you seen Luisa?
I am seeing Luisa.

GRAMÁTICA

¿Qué pasa?

¿Qué pasa? – What's wrong? is probably one the phrases you will most frequently hear in Spain. The phrase *¿qué pasa?*, is used when someone wants to know what's wrong or what's happened. The phrase is also often used when greeting someone informally: Hola, Ana, *¿qué pasa?* – Hello, Ana, how goes it? The doctor does not use the phrase *¿qué pasa?*, but uses *¿qué le pasa?* instead (literally: what is happening to you?). If he were to use the informal form of address with Ana, he would say *¿que te pasa?*
Instead of saying *estoy* enfermo you can also use *estoy malo/mala* (but not *soy malo/mala*). We have already explained the difference between the verbs *ser* and *estar* in lesson VI. *Estoy malo* refers to a temporary state "I am ill" or "I don't feel good". The form *soy malo*, on the other hand, refers to a basic character attribute: "I am a bad person".

The Demonstrative Pronouns

The demonstrative pronoun has three different forms which depend on how far away the speaker is from the object he is referring to:
este for anything which is close to the speaker,
ese for anything which is not quite so close to the speaker and
aquel for anything which is relatively far away from the speaker.

Examples:

Yo compro este libro. — I buy this book (here).
Antonio compra ese libro. — Antonio buys that book (over there).
Rita compra aquel libro. — Dolores buys that book (over there at the back).

The plural forms are:
> *estos*
> *esos*
> *aquellos*

Examples:
> *Yo compro estos libros.*
> *Antonio compra esos libros.*
> *Dolores compra aquellos libros.*

Este, ese and *aquel* are the masculine forms. The feminine forms are:
> *esta*
> *esa*
> *aquella*

Examples:
> *Yo quiero esta camisa.*
> *Antonio quiere esa camisa.*
> *Dolores quiere aquella camisa.*

An –s is also added here in the plural.

Examples:
> *Yo quiero estas camisas.*
> *Antonio quiere esas camisas.*
> *Dolores quiere aquellas camisas.*

Supplementary Exercise 1
We will name various items which are very close to you. You must say that you want them.

Example: unos zapatos; Quiero estos zapatos.
1. unos zapatos;
2. una chaqueta;
3. un jersey;
4. unas galletas.

Now imagine that you are at the greengrocer's and that the items mentioned are not quite so close to you. Proceed as in the previous exercise.

Example: las patatas; Quiero esas patatas.
5. las patatas;
6. los tomates;
7. la lechuga;
8. el pimiento.

Imagine that you want to speak to various people who are relatively far away from you.

Example: un señor; Quiero hablar con aquel señor.
9. un señor;
10. unos señores;
11. una señora;
12. unas señoras.

The Perfect

To form the perfect in Spanish, the auxiliary verb _haber_ (to have) and the past participle of the verb is used as in English:

I **have knocked** myself.
Me **he dado** un golpe.

When forming the past participle, a distinction must be made between verbs ending in -_ar_ and verbs ending in -_er_ and -_ir_.

For verbs ending in –_ar_, -_ado_ is added to the root of the verb:

comprar	compr-ado
hablar	habl-ado
visitar	visit-ado

he comprado	I have bought
he hablado	I have spoken
he visitado	I have visited

For verbs ending in *–er* and *-ir, -ido* is added to the root of the verb:

beber	beb-ido
comer	com-ido
querer	quer-ido

he bebido	I have drunk
he comido	I have eaten
he querido	I have wanted / loved

vivir	-	viv-ido
venir	-	ven-ido
dormir	-	dorm-ido

he vivido	I have lived
he venido	I have come
he dormido	I have slept

Irregular forms:

decir	(to say)	dicho; he dicho	I have said
hacer	(to do)	hecho; he hecho	I have done
escribir	(to write)	escrito; he escrito	I have written
ver	(to see)	visto; he visto	I have seen

The other persons in the singular and plural of the auxiliary verb *haber* are:

		HABER (Present)
	1. Pers.	he
Singular	2. Pers.	has
	3. Pers.	ha
	1. Pers.	hemos
Plural	2. Pers.	habéis
	3. Pers.	han

yo	⇒	He comprado un libro.
tú	⇒	Has comprado unos pantalones.
él/ella	⇒	Ha comprado una camisa.
nosotros	⇒	Hemos comprado fruta.
vosotros	⇒	Habéis comprado perfume.
ellos	⇒	Han comprado discos.

The Use of the Perfect:
The perfect is used more often in Spanish to refer to the past than it is in English. Spanish also uses two other forms of the past. We will look at these later.

Algún

The word *algún* (any or some or one) when it appears without a noun is treated in exactly the same way as the indefinite article *un*:

algún	+	masculine singular noun	⇒	*alguno*
alguna	+	feminine singular noun	⇒	*alguna*
algunos	+	masculine plural noun	⇒	*algunos*
algunas	+	feminine plural noun	⇒	*algunas*

Examples:

¿Conoces algún hotel?	Do you know any hotel?
Sí, conozco alguno.	Yes, I know one.
¿Conoces alguna pensión?	Do you know any guest house?
Sí, conozco alguna.	Yes, I know one.
¿Conoces algunos restaurantes?	Do you know any restaurants?
Sí, conozco algunos.	Yes, I know some.
¿Conoces algunas ciudades españolas?	Do you know any Spanish cities?
Sí, conozco algunas.	Yes, I know some.

Supplementary Exercise 2
Ask if the person you are talking to has any of the items mentioned.

Example: pantalones; ¿Tienes algunos pantalones?
1. pantalones;
2. jersey;
3. dinero;
4. tarjeta de crédito.

The Continuous Form

The continuous verb form is used a lot in Spanish to express the continuous nature of an action:

jugando   "playing"

Example:
Jugando al baloncesto me   Whilst playing basketball I (have)
he doblado la mano.   twisted my hand.

The continuous form of verbs ending in *-ar* is formed by adding *-ando* to the root of the verb:

jugar	jug-ando
bailar	bail-ando
cantar	cant-ando

I am playing – *estoy jugando*
To express that someone is in the process of doing something, the verb *estar* and the continuous verb form are used:

to be doing something   =   ESTAR + continuous form

estoy bailando   I am dancing
estoy cantando   I am singing

The continuous form of verbs ending in _–er_ is formed by adding _–iendo_
to the root of the verb:

comer	com-iendo
beber	beb-iendo
doler	dol-iendo

estoy comiendo	I am eating
estoy bebiendo	I am drinking
me está doliendo	It is hurting me

The verb _leer_ (to read) is irregular:
| _estoy leyendo_ | I am reading. |

The continuous form of verbs ending in _–ir_ is also formed by adding
–iendo to the root of the verb:

vivir	viv-iendo
escribir	escrib-iendo
subir	sub-iendo

estoy viviendo	I am living
estoy escribiendo	I am writing
estoy subiendo	I am going up (to another floor)

The verbs _oír_ (to listen / to hear) and **_dormir_** (to sleep) are irregular:
| _estoy oyendo_ | I am listening |
| _estoy durmiendo_ | I am sleeping. |

The continuous form can also be formed using the verb **_seguir_** instead
of the verb **_estar_**:

to carry on eating = **SEGUIR + continuous form**

sigo comiendo	carry on eating / I continue to eat
sigo leyendo I	carry on reading
sigo durmiendo	I carry on sleeping

The verb *seguir* is conjugated in the same way as the verb *vestir* (lesson IV), i.e. by modifying the root vowel:

		SEGUIR (Present)
	1. Pers.	*sigo*
Singular	2. Pers.	*sigues*
	3. Pers.	*sigue*
	1. Pers.	*seguimos*
Plural	2. Pers.	*seguís*
	3. Pers.	*siguen*

Supplementary Exercise 3
Say that those mentioned below are continuing to sleep

Example: Ana; Sigue durmiendo.
1. Ana;
2. nosotros;
3. tú;
4. los niños.

Relative Clauses using *that*

Subordinate relative clauses introduced by the conjunction *que* (that) are straightforward. The word order remains the same as it does in English. Look at the following sentences:
Examples:

Estoy embarazada.	⇒	*Creo que estoy embarazada.*
I am pregnant.	⇒	I think that I am pregnant.
Está enfermo.	⇒	*Creo que está enfermo.*
He is ill.	⇒	I think that he is ill.
Tiene mucha fiebre.	⇒	*Creo que tiene mucha fiebre.*
He has a high fever.	⇒	I think that he has a high fever.

If the speaker wants to express a degree of doubt or a wish or desire, then subordinate relative clauses using *that* are more difficult to form. In such cases the dependent verb must appear in the subjunctive form. We will look at this topic later on.

Supplementary Exercise 4

Say that you think the following statements apply.
Example: Tengo mucha fiebre. Creo que tengo mucha fiebre.
1. Tengo mucha fiebre.
2. Matilde está embarazada.
3. Miguel está enfermo.
4. Los niños están malos.

Vocabulary

La garganta is the word used to mean "the throat" and
el cuello refers to "the neck".

Instead of saying *me duele la cabeza,* you can also say
tengo dolor de cabeza – I have a headache.
Types of pain which people most complain about:

Headache	*dolor de cabeza*
Stomach ache	*dolor de barriga*
Backache	*dolor de espalda*
A sore throat	*dolor de garganta*

Toothache – *dolor de muelas*
In Spanish a distinction is made between the incisors and the
molars. *El diente* means the tooth in general, *la muela* refers to the
molars. Hence *El dolor de muelas* literally means "pain of the
molars".

Earache – *dolor de oídos*
In Spanish a distinction is made between the inner and outer ears.
El oído is used to refer to the inner ear and one's hearing. *La oreja* is
the external part of the ear.

Supplementary Exercise 5

**Repeat the names used to describe the following specialists.
Perhaps you can guess the fourth example.**

Example: el médico para mujeres; El médico para mujeres se llama el ginecólogo.
1.   el médico para mujeres;
2.   el médico para niños;
3.   el médico para los dientes;
4.   el médico para los animales.

Information about the Country

In Spain people tend to complain sooner and more frequently about pain. So
don't hold back when you're at the doctor's. He might think that there isn't much
wrong with you!

Solutions to the Supplementary Exercises

Supplementary Exercise 1

1.   Quiero estos zapatos.
2.   Quiero esta chaqueta.
3.   Quiero este jersey.
4.   Quiero estas galletas.

5.   Quiero esas patatas.
6.   Quiero esos tomates.
7.   Quiero esa lechuga.
8.   Quiero ese pimiento.

9.   Quiero hablar con aquel señor.
10. Quiero hablar con aquellos señores.
11. Quiero hablar con aquella señora.
12. Quiero hablar con aquellas señoras.

Supplementary Exercise 2

1. ¿Tienes algunos pantalones?
2. ¿Tienes algún jersey?
3. ¿Tienes algún dinero?
4. ¿Tienes alguna tarjeta de crédito?

Supplementary Exercise 3

1. Sigue durmiendo.
2. Seguimos durmiendo.
3. Sigues durmiendo.
4. Siguen durmiendo.

Supplementary Exercise 4

1. Creo que tengo mucha fiebre.
2. Creo que Matilde está embarazada.
3. Creo que Miguel está enfermo.
4. Creo que los niños están malos.

Supplementary Exercise 5

1. El médico para mujeres se llama el ginecólogo.
2. El médico para niños se llama el pediatra.
3. El médico para los dientes se llama dentista.
4. El médico para los animales se llama veterinario.

In this lesson you will learn how to:

- express yourself in traffic situations
- say something is not allowed
- express surprise or annoyance

CD3
TOP 1 Remember the following expressions or phrases:

todo el mundo	everybody, everyone (literally: all the world)
el agente de tráfico	the traffic policeman
Empieza a trabajar a las ocho.	He starts to work a 8 o'clock.
Hay muchos problemas de tráfico.	There are a lot of traffic problems.
Hay demasiados coches.	There are too many cars.
su documentación, por favor	Your papers please
Déjeme su carnet de	Give me (lit: Let to me) your identity card.
el carnet de conducir	the driving licence
la documentación del vehículo	vehicle logbook
Aquí tiene.	Here you are.
Puede continuar.	You can continue.
Retire el vehículo.	Move the vehicle.
Aquí está prohibido aparcar.	Parking is prohibited here.
Aquí no se puede aparcar.	You can't park here.
Prohibido fumar.	No smoking.
Prohibido adelantar.	No overtaking.
Prohibido el paso.	No entry.
Ceda el paso.	Give way.
¿Cuál es su coche?	Which is your car?

Se lo ha llevado la grúa.	It has been towed away.
Es zona de carga y descarga.	This is a loading and unloading area.
Ha pasado el límite de velocidad.	You have exceeded the speed limit
La multa es de veinte mil Pesetas.	The fine is 20,000 pesetas.
¡Qúe barbaridad!	How outrageous!
¡Es increíble!	That's incredible!, I don't believe it.
¡Vaya!	*Exclamation similar to:* Well, I never!
¡Hombre!	*Mild explitive equivalent to*: Damn!, Oh blast it!
¡No puede ser!	That's not possible (lit: that can't be)!

CD3 TOP2 **DIÁLOGOS**

The story: In this lesson we join Don José at work.

Narrator

Don José es policía. Vive y trabaja en Marbella, en la Costa del Sol. Don José es agente de tráfico. Empieza a trabajar a las ocho de la mañana. Primero, va a la oficina, donde se reúnen todos los agentes del mismo turno. Luego, sale con su compañera Maite a controlar el tráfico. En Marbella, como en casi todas las ciudades españolas, hay muchos problemas de tráfico, porque hay demasiados coches.

Don José is a policeman. He lives and works in Marbella on the Costa del Sol. Don José is a traffic policeman. He starts work at 8 o'clock in the morning. First of all he goes to the office where all the policemen on the same shift meet. Then he goes with his colleague Maite out on traffic duty (lit: to control the traffic). In Marbella, as in nearly all Spanish cities, there are a lot of traffic problems because there are too many cars.

Contents: Don José at work

José
Por favor, su documentación.

Your papers please.

Driver
Aquí tiene mi carnet de identidad.

Here is my identity card.

José
Déjeme también su carnet de conducir y la documentación del vehículo.

Let me see your driving licence and the car logbook.

Driver
Aquí tiene.

Here you are.

José
Muchas gracias. Puede continuar.

Thank you. You may continue.

José
Por favor, retire el vehículo, aquí está prohibido aparcar.

Please move the vehicle. Parking is prohibited here.

Driver
Vaya.

Well, I never!

Driver
Perdone, ¿dónde está mi coche?

Excuse me, where is my car?

José
¿Cuál es su coche?

Which is your car?

Driver
Un Seat Cupra rojo que estaba aquí.

A red Seat Cupra which was here.

José
Ah, sí, se lo ha llevado la grúa.

Oh yes, it's been towed away.

Driver
¡No puede ser!

That's impossible!

José
Hombre, esto es zona de carga
y descarga.

Now listen here, this is a loading
area.

José
Buenos días. Ha sobrepasado usted el
límite de velocidad. La multa es de
veinte mil pesetas.

Good morning, You have
exceeded the speed limit. The fine is
20,000 pesetas.

Driver
¿Qué barbaridad! Veinte mil pesetas.
Es increíble. ... Aquí tiene.

That's outrageous! 20,000 pesetas.
I don't believe it. Here you are.

B: EJERCICIOS

Ejercicio 1:
Diga que empieza a hacerlo. – Say that you are starting to do something.

E Ejemplo – Example:

Voz: *Don José está controlando el tráfico.*
Don José is controlling the traffic.

Usted: *Don José empieza a controlar el tráfico.*
Don José starts to control the traffic.

Voz: *Don José empieza a controlar el tráfico.*

Usted: *Don José empieza a controlar el tráfico.*

Y ahora usted, por favor – and now you:

1. Don José está controlando el
tráfico.
Don José empieza a controlar
el tráfico.

   Don José is controlling
the traffic.
Don José starts to control
the traffic.

2. Alfonso y Francisco están
visitando la ciudad de Granada.
Alfonso y Francisco empiezan a
visitar la ciudad de Granada.

   Alfonso and Francisco are visiting
the city of Granada.
Alfonso and Francisco start to visit
the city of Granada.

3. Miguel se está afeitando.
Miguel empieza a afeitarse.

   Miguel is shaving.
Miguel starts to shave.

4. Don Juan y doña María están
desayunando.
Don Juan y doña María empiezan
a desayunar.

   Don Juan and Doña María are having
breakfast.
Don Juan and Doña María start to have
breakfast.

5. Estoy trabajando.
Empiezo a trabajar.

   I am working.
I start to work.

6. Estamos comiendo una paella.
Empezamos a comer una paella.

   We are eating paella.
We start to eat paella.

7. Estáis hablando con el médico.
Empezáis a hablar con el médico.

   We are speaking to the doctor.
We start to speak to the doctor.

Ejercicio 2:

Diga que tienen que hacerlo – Say that they have to do it.

E Ejemplo – Example:

Voz: *No quiero ir a Madrid.*
I don't want to go to Madrid.

Usted: *Tienes que ir a Madrid.*
You have to go to Madrid.

Voz: *Tienes que ir a Madrid.*

Usted: *Tienes que ir a Madrid.*

Y ahora usted, por favor – and now you:

1. No quiero ir a Madrid.
   Tienes que ir a Madrid.

   I don't want to go to Madrid.
   You have to go to Madrid.

2. Los niños no quieren ir a la escuela.
   Tienen que ir a la escuela.

   The children don't want to go
   to school.
   They have to go to school.

3. Los policías no quieren regular
   el tráfico.
   Tienen que regular el tráfico.

   The policemen don't want to
   control the traffic.
   They have to control the traffic.

4. Los estudiantes no quieren
   levantarse temprano.
   Tienen que levantarse temprano.

   The students don't want to get up
   early.
   They have to get up early.

5. Isabelita no quiere dormir.
   Tiene que dormir.

   Isabelita doesn't want to sleep.
   She has to sleep.

6. No quiero comer fruta.
   Tienes que comer fruta.

   I don't want to eat any fruit.
   You have to eat some fruit.

7. No queremos ir al dentista.
   Tenéis que ir al dentista.

   We don't want to go to the dentist.
   You have to go to the dentist.

CD3 TOP5 **Ejercicio 3:**

Todos estaban en casa – Say that they were at home.

E **Ejemplo – Example:**

Voz:	*yo*
	I
Usted:	*Estaba en casa.*
	I was at home.
Voz:	*Estaba en casa.*
Usted:	*Estaba en casa.*

 Y ahora usted, por favor – and now you:

1. yo
   Estaba en casa.   I was at home.

2. María y los niños   María and the children
   Estaban en casa.   (They) were at home.

3. mi hermano   My brother.
   Estaba en casa.   He was at home.

4. yo y mis hermanos   (Me) I and my brothers and sisters.
   Estábamos en casa.   We were at home.

5. tú   You.
   Estabas en casa.   You were at home.

6. mi mujer   My wife.
   Estaba en casa   She was at home.

7. tú y tu familia   You and your family.
   Estabais en casa.   You were at home.

Ejercicio 4:

Add similar qualifying statements.

E **Ejemplo – Example:**

Voz: *En Marbella hay muchos problemas de tráfico.*
In Marbella there are a lot of traffic problems.

Usted: *En Marbella, como en casi todas las ciudades,*
hay muchos problemas de tráfico.
In Marbella, as in nearly all cities,
there are a lot of traffic problems.

Voz: *En Marbella, como en casi todas las ciudades,*
hay muchos problemas de tráfico.

Usted: *En Marbella, como en casi todas las ciudades,*
hay muchos problemas de tráfico.

 Y ahora usted, por favor – and now you:

1. En Marbella hay muchos problemas de tráfico.
En Marbella, como en casi todas las ciudades, hay muchos problemas de tráfico.

In Marbella there are a lot of traffic problems.
In Marbella, as in nearly all cities, there are a lot of traffic problems.

2. En el Hotel Meliá hay un restaurante.
   En el hotel Meliá, como en casi todos los hoteles, hay un restaurante.

   In the Hotel Meliá there is a restaurant.
   In the Hotel Meliá, as in nearly all hotels, there is a restaurant.

3. En Marbella hay un hospital.
   En Marbella, como en casi todas las ciudades, hay un hospital.

   In Marbella there is a hospital.
   In Marbella, as in nearly all cities, there is a hospital.

4. En la provincia de Gerona hay montañas.
   En la provincia de Gerona, como en casi todas las provincias, hay montañas.

   In the province of Gerona there are mountains.
   In the province of Gerona, as in nearly all provinces, there are mountains.

5. En la frutería LOLI hay plátanos.

   En la frutería LOLI, como en casi todas las fruterías, hay plátanos.

   At LOLI's fruit shop there are bananas.
   At LOLI's fruit shop, as in nearly all fruit shops, there are bananas.

6. En la Universidad de Granada hay muchos estudiantes.
   En la Universidad de Granada, como en casi todas las universidades, hay muchos estudiantes.

   At the University of Granada there are a lot of students.
   At the University of Granada, as at nearly all universities, there are a lot of students.

7. En el centro de la ciudad de Barcelona hay muchos taxis.
   En el centro de la ciudad de Barcelona, como en casi todas las ciudades, hay muchos taxis.

   In the centre of the city of Barcelona there are a lot of taxis.
   In the centre of the city of Barcelona, as in nearly all cities, there are a lot of taxis.

GRAMÁTICA

Empezar a hacer algo

The verb *empezar a* + infinitive (to start to do something) is conjugated like the verb *sentarse*, i.e. with changes to the root vowel in the singular and the third person plural.

Examples:

Empiezo a trabajar.	I start to work.
Empezamos a conducir.	We start to drive.
Don José empieza a trabajar a las ocho de la mañana.	Don José starts to work at 8 o'clock in the morning.

El mismo – la misma

Like all other adjectives *mismo* changes its ending to agree with the noun:

el mismo hombre   *la misma mujer*

los mismos hombres   *las mismas mujeres*

Supplementary Exercise 1
Say that you have the same thing.

Example: Tengo un libro de Saramago. Yo tengo el mismo.
1. Tengo un libro de Saramago.
2. Tengo tres balones blancos de fútbol.
3. Tengo una camisa de colores de Adidas.
4. Tengo unos vaqueros negros de algodón.

Todo – toda

The word **todo** (all, all of or whole) agrees with the noun in gender and number.

todos los hombres	all men (or all people)
todas las mujeres	all women
todo el dinero	all of the money
toda la tarde	the whole afternoon

Example:

En Marbella, como en casi todas las ciudades españolas, hay muchos problemas de tráfico.	In Marbella, as in nearly all Spanish cities, there are a lot of traffic problems.

The phrase **todo el mundo** (literally: all of the world) means "everyone" or "everybody".

Example:

Pablo habla con todo el mundo.	Pablo speaks to everyone.

On its own **todo** means "everything"".

Example:

Todo está bien.	Everything 's OK.

Supplementary Exercise 2

In the following exercise you will be asked if you want to have something. Reply by saying you want all of it.

Example: ¿Quiere sacar dinero? Quiero sacar todo el dinero.

1. ¿Quiere sacar dinero?
2. ¿Quiere cambiar los euros en pesetas?
3. ¿Quiere visitar las ciudades españolas?
4. ¿Quiere comerse la fruta?

Demasiado

You have already met the word ***demasiado*** in lesson 2:

Un restaurante de cuatro tenedores   A "four fork" restaurant
es demasiado caro.   is too expensive.

In this sentence the word ***demasiado*** does not change because it is being used as an adverb. Similar compounds:

demasiado pequeño   *demasiado elegante*
demasiado claro   *demasiado frío*
demasiado caliente

In each of these cases ***demasiado*** is translated by "too":

demasiado pequeño   too small
demasiado elegante   too elegant
demasiado claro   too light
demasiado frío   too cold
demasiado caliente   too hot

When ***demasiado*** is used as an adjective, its ending changes to agree in gender and number with the noun, as is the case for all other adjectives:

*demasiad**o** tráfico*
*demasiad**a** cerveza*
*demasiad**os** coches*
*demasiad**as** casas*

In each of these cases, the meaning of

demasiado   is "too much or too many".
demasiado tráfico   too much traffic
demasiada cerveza   too much beer
demasiados coches   too many cars
demasiadas casas   too many houses

Example:
Hay muchos problemas de tráfico,   There are a lot of traffic problems
porque hay demasiados coches.   because there are too many cars.

Supplementary Exercise 3
Now say there is too much of what is mentioned.

Example: problemas; Hay demasiados problemas.
1. problemas;
2. tráfico;
3. hoteles;
4. mosquitos.

Por qué/Porque – Why and because

Porque means "because", *por qué* means "why":

¿Por qué no vienes?	Why aren't you coming?
Porque no tengo coche.	Because I don't have a car.
¿Por qué no compras un coche?	Why don't you buy a car?
Porque no tengo dinero.	Because I haven't any money.
¿Por qué visitas España?	Why are you visiting Spain?
Porque me gusta mucho el sur.	Because I love the Mediterranean (the south).

Supplementary Exercise 4
Now say why you can't do something. You're not hungry, thirsty, you don't have any money and you aren't tired.

Example: ¿Por qué no duermes? – Porque no tengo sueño.
1. ¿Por qué no duermes?
2. ¿Por qué no comes?
3. ¿Por qué no bebes?
4. ¿Por qué no compras un piso?

Caution: The interrogative form is often used in Spanish to politely tell someone to do something:

¿Por qué no comes?	Why don't you eat something! (Go on eat something)
¿Por qué no bebes?	Why don't you drink something! (Go on drink something)

It would, of course, be completely wrong to reply in these cases using the word *because*. You either accept the invitation by saying thank you or you politely decline the offer.

¿Por qué no comes?	Go on, eat something!
Sí, gracias.	OK, thank you.
¿Por qué no bebes?	Go on, drink something!
Gracias, no tengo sed.	Thank you, but I am not thirsty.

Tener que hacer algo

In Spanish the construction *tener que hacer algo* means "to have to do something"

$$\textbf{\textit{tener que}} \; + \; \textbf{infinitive}$$

Examples:

Tengo que irme.	I have to go.
Juan tiene que dormir.	Juan has to sleep.
Tenemos que pagar la cuenta.	We have to pay the bill.
Don José tiene que regular la circulación	Don José has to control the traffic.

Nouns Ending in -tor

The word **conductor** (driver) is formed by adding **-tor** to the root of the verb **conducir**:

$$\textbf{conduc} \; + \; \textbf{tor}$$

Other nouns are also formed using the same pattern:

escribir	to write
el escritor	the writer
dirigir	to conduct or direct
el director	the conductor or the director
elegir	to vote
el elector	the voter

185

producir	to manufacture or produce
el productor	the manufacturer or producer
traducir	to translate
el traductor	the translator

Indirect Object Personal Pronouns

The indirect object first person singular personal pronoun *me* is the same as the equivalent reflexive pronoun in the first person singular. In the plural they are also the same:

me ducho		
me afeito	AND	*me dejas el carnet*
nos duchamos		
nos afeitamos	AND	*nos dejas el carnet*

The second person forms are also identical:

te duchas		
te afeitas	AND	*te dejo el carnet*
os ducháis		
os afeitáis	AND	*os dejo el carnet*

It is only in the third person that the indirect object personal pronouns differ from the equivalent reflexive pronouns:

se ducha		
se afeita	BUT	*le dejo el carnet*
se duchan		
se afeitan	BUT	*les dejo el carnet*

INDIRECT OBJECT PERSONAL PRONOUNS

		SUBJECT	INDIRECT OBJECT	
	1. Pers.	yo	*me*	(to me)
Singular	2. Pers.	tú	*te*	(to you)
	3. Pers.	él	*le*	(to you)
		ella	*le*	(to him)
		usted	*le*	(to her)
	1. Pers.	nosotros	*no*s	(to us)
Plural	2. Pers.	vosotros	*os*	(to you)
	3. Pers.	ellos	*les*	(to them)
		ellas	*les*	(to them)
		ustedes	*les*	(to you)

Example:

Déjeme su carnet de conducir	literally: let to me your driving licence
	(Give (to) **me** (indirect object)
	your driving licence)

¿Cuál?

The interrogative pronoun *cuál* does not change its form to agree with the gender of the word it refers to:

¿Cuál es su mujer?	Which is your wife?
¿Cuál es su marido?	Which is your husband?

If the word being referred to is in the plural then *cuál* becomes *cuáles*:

¿Cuáles son tus hijos?	Which are your sons?
¿Cuáles son tus hijas?	Which are your daughters?

Example:

Perdone, ¿Dónde está mi coche?	Excuse me, where is my car?
¿Cuál es su coche?	Which is your car?

The "imperfecto"

The complexity of Spanish tenses is similar to that of English. For the past tenses there is the present perfect which is normally used if the action or a consequence of the action is related in some way to the present from the speaker's point of view. e. g.

he comido	I have eaten
	which more or less means
	"I am now full up" or
ha venido mi amigo	my friend has come
	which roughly means
	"My friend is now here".

Apart form the present perfect there are two other tenses used for the simple past – the so-called "imperfecto" and the "indefinido". The "imperfecto" is used for actions which are seen to have been going on in the past. The "indefinido" is used for actions which were completed in the past. There is often an overlap between the "imperfecto" and "indefinido", and, in many cases, both forms can be used depending on what the speaker is intending to say. Experience shows that the correct use of the tenses only comes about after a longer stay in a country where Spanish is spoken. So for the moment you must be patient.

The verb *estar* is conjugated in the "imperfecto" as follows:

		ESTAR (Imperfecto)
	1. Pers.	*estaba*
Singular	2. Pers.	*estabas*
	3. Pers.	*estaba*
	1. Pers.	*estábamos*
Pluria	2. Pers.	*estabaiis*
	3. Pers.	*estaban*

The "imperfecto" forms only differ from the present in that the syllable -*ba*- is inserted between the root of the verb and its ending. The only exception to this is in the first person singular.

Example:

Un Seat Cupra rojo que estaba aquí.   A red Seat Cupra which was here.

Vocabulary

El agente

The word *agente* has various meanings such as: agent, representative, mediator, clerk, civil servant and public employee. *Agente de tráfico* is a traffic policeman (literally: traffic agent).
Some other compounds using *agente* which you should know:

el agente de policía	policeman
el agente comercial	commercial traveller or representative
el agente inmobiliario	estate agent
el agente secreto	secret agent

La oficina

La oficina is another term which can have a number of different meanings: public office, office, chamber (lawyer) and workshop. You have already come across the term *oficina de correos* – the post office.

Here are some other compounds using *oficina* which you should know:

oficina central	head office
oficina de empleo	job centre / employment exchange

Identity Cards and Papers

La documentación is the word used to refer to identity papers and documents. *Los papeles* is a popular alternative to this. *El carnet de identidad* is the identity card. The abbreviation *D.N.I.* is often used for this (short for *Documento Nacional de Identidad*). *El carnet de conducir* is the driving licence, *el pasaporte* the passport.

Example:

Don José:	*Por favor, su documentación.*
conductor:	*Aquí tiene mi carnet de identidad.*
Don José:	*Déjeme también su carnet de conducir y la documentación del vehículo.*

189

Continuar

The verb *continuar* means "to continue" or "to carry on".

Examples:

Don José: - *Muchas gracias.*	Thank you.
Puede continuar.	You may continue.
La secretaria está escribiendo una carta.	She can carry on writing.
Puede continuar.	
Julia está estudiando.	She can continue studying.
Puede continuar.	
Ester está comiendo.	She can carry on eating.
Puede continuar.	
Estamos caminando.	You can carry on walking.
Podéis continuar.	

Retirar algo

Retirar algo means, depending on context, "to withdraw something" or "to remove something".

Example:

Por favor, retire el vehículo, aquí está	Please remove the vehicle.
prohibido aparcar	Parking is prohibited here.
Retiro mi pregunta.	I withdraw my question.
Retiro mi protesta.	I withdraw my objection.
Me retiro.	I withdraw.
Nos retiramos.	We withdraw.

Conveying the Notion that Something Is Prohibited

Está prohibido.	It is forbidden.
Aquí está prohibido aparcar.	Parking is prohibited here.
prohibir	to prohibit, forbid
prohibido	prohibited, forbidden
está prohibido	it is prohibited
está prohibido aparcar	parking prohibited

Other things which are often not permitted:

smoking	fumar

talking loudly	*hablar en voz alta*
touching something	*tocar*
eating inside a building	*comer en un edificio*
overtaking	*adelantar*

In many cases the following simple forms are used instead of *está prohibido*
NO FUMAR
NO HABLAR EN VOZ ALTA
NO TOCAR

Example:

Ha sobrepasado usted el límite de velocidad.	You have exceeded the speed limit.

Other limits or thresholds which should not be transgressed:

Alcohol limit	*el nivel de alcohol permitido*
Noise threshold	*el nivel de ruidos permitido*
Time limit	*el límite de tiempo*

You should definitely know the following traffic signs:

PROHIBIDO APARCAR	SE LLAMA GRÚA
Parking prohibited	Vehicles will be towed away

PROHIBIDO ADELANTAR
No overtaking

PROHIBIDO EL PASO
No entry

PELIGRO DESVÍO PROVISIONAL
Caution (literally: danger) diversion

CINTURON DE SEGURIDAD OBLIGATORIO
Wearing of seatbelts mandatory

SALIDA	ENTRADA
Exit	Entrance

CEDA EL PASO
Give way

CARRETERA EN OBRAS	CALLE CORTADA
Roadworks	Road closed

In Spanish a precise distinction is made between *la carretera* (the road linking two towns) and *la calle* (the street/road within a town or city). *La autopista* is the word for motorway for which you still have to pay a toll to use. *La autovía* is an express road similar to a motorway which you don't have to pay to use. *El camino* is used to mean "a country road" or "track".

Vehicles

Don José controla los vehículos.	Don José checks the vehicles.

The most common vehicles are:

el coche	the car
el camión	the lorry
la motocicleta or just *la moto*	the motorbike or moped
la bicicleta or just *la bici*	the bicycle

The most common forms of public transport are:

el taxi	the taxi
el autobús	the bus
el tren	the train
el metro	the tube, underground train
el avión	the aeroplane

Solutions to the Supplementary Exercises

Supplementary Exercise 1

1. Yo tengo el mismo.
2. Yo tengo los mismos.
3. Yo tengo la misma.
4. Yo tengo los mismos.

Supplementary Exercise 2

1. Quiero sacar todo el dinero.
2. Quiero cambiar todos los euros en pesetas.
3. Quiero visitar todas las ciudades españolas.
4. Quiero comerme toda la fruta.

Supplementary Exercise 3

1. Hay demasiados problemas.
2. Hay demasiado tráfico.
3. Hay demasiados hoteles.
4. Hay demasiados mosquitos.

Supplementary Exercise 4

1. Porque no tengo sueño.
2. Porque no tengo hambre.
3. Porque no tengo sed.
4. Porque no tengo dinero.

LECCIÓN 10

Planeando las vacaciones

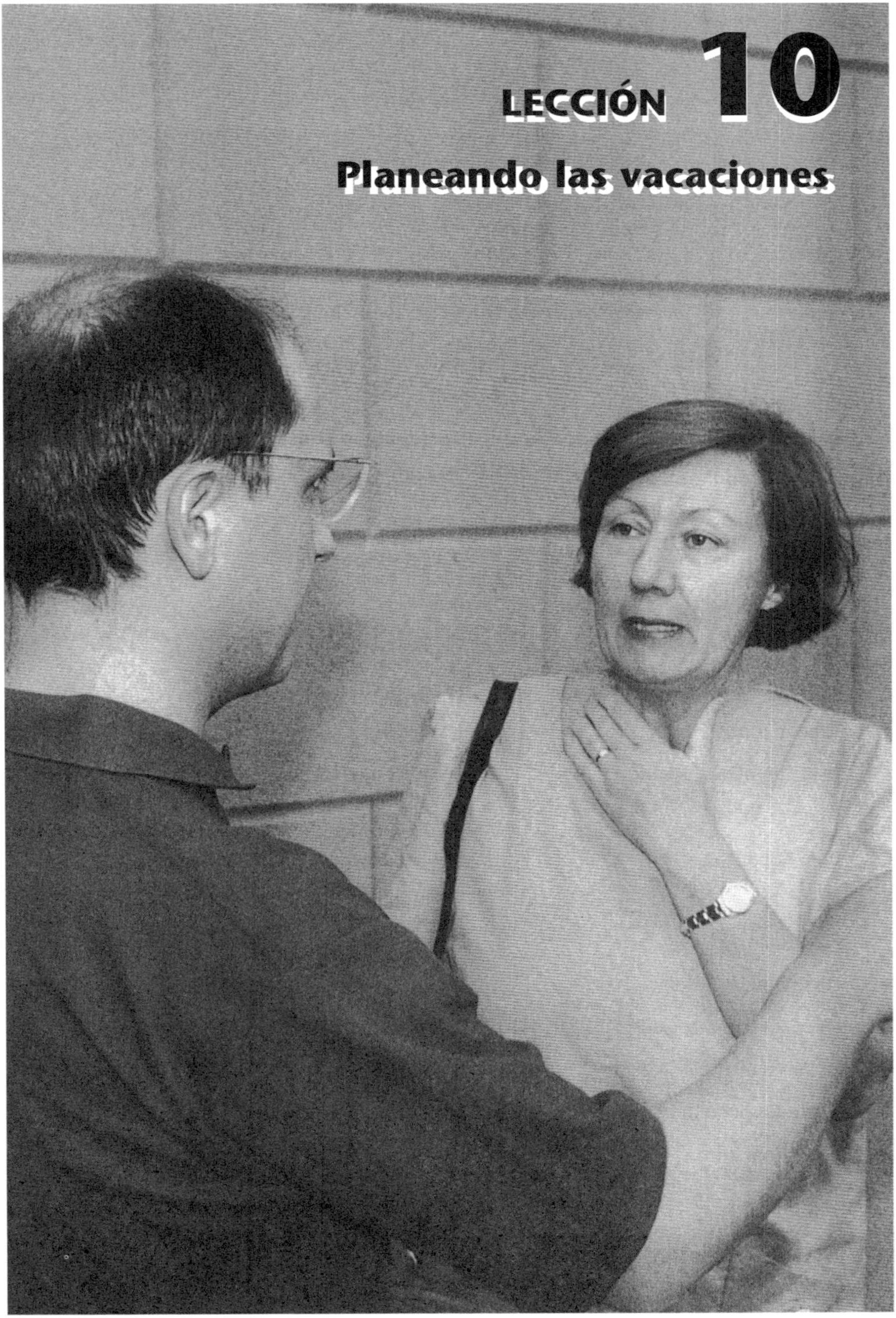

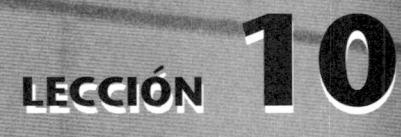

In this lesson you will learn how to:

- talk about the weather
- describe a place
- request something in the negative

CD3 TOP7 Remember the following expressions and phrases:

Quieren ir de vacaciones a la playa.	They want to have a holiday at the beach.
la familia del hermano de don José	the family of Don José's brother
una reunión familiar	a family reunion / get together
el año pasado	last year
el año anterior	the previous year
el año que viene	next year
Estoy de acuerdo contigo.	I agree with you.
En el norte no hace tanto calor.	In the north it's not so hot.
Llueve todo el día.	It rains all day long.
Hace un día espléndido.	It's a wonderful day.
Luce el sol.	The sun shines.
Está nublado.	It is cloudy.
Hace frío.	It is cold.
Hace calor.	It is warm.
Hace mucho calor.	It is hot.
Hace un frío que pela.	It is bitterly cold.
Hace viento.	It is windy.
Corre un poco de viento.	There's a light breeze.
Está lloviendo.	It's raining.

Está lloviendo a cántaros.	It's pouring buckets (literally: in jugs).
Está nevando.	It's snowing.
Hay tormenta.	There's a storm.
como siempre en esta época	as always at this time of year
Hoy es el día veinte de enero.	Today is the 20th of January.
No seáis tontos.	Don't be silly.
Todo el mundo sabe hablar español.	Everyone speaks Spanish.
Es verdad.	That's right.
Es bueno conocer otros sitios.	It's good to get to know other areas.
La gente es encantadora.	The people are charming.
Podemos alquilar un piso en la playa.	We can rent a flat on the beach.
Se lo están pasando bomba.	They have a lot of fun.
desde luego	certainly/yes, of course

A: DIÁLOGOS

Narrator

Durante el mes de agosto don José
y su familia quieren ir de vacaciones
a la playa. Como siempre, quieren ir
con la familia del hermano de don
José. En una reunión familiar
discuten sus planes.

In August Don José and his family
would like to spend their holidays
at the beach. As always they want
to go with the family of Don José's
brother. At a family get together
they discuss their plans.

José

Vamos a ver. El año pasado estuvimos
en la Costa del Sol y el año anterior
en la Costa Brava. Este año quiero ver
otras partes de España. En el norte
también hay playas maravillosas.

Look, last year we went to the Costa
del Sol and the previous year to the
Costa Brava. This year I would like
to see some other parts of Spain.
In the north there are also some
marvellous beaches.

Adelina

Desde luego. Estoy de acuerdo contigo.
Yo también quiero conocer otros sitios.
Y además, en el norte no hace tanto
calor.

Of course. I agree with you. I would
also like to get to know some other
areas. And what's more, in the
north it's not so hot.

Jesús

¡Sí, y llueve todo el día!

Yes and it rains all day long!

Maira

Es cierto, y además no sabemos
hablar ni gallego ni vasco.

That's true and we also can't speak
either Gallician or Basque.

Ramón

Niños, no seáis tontos. En el norte,
todo el mundo sabe hablar español.
El gallego o el vasco, lo hablan sólo
entre ellos.

Children, don't be silly. In the north
everyone speaks Spanish. They
only speak Gallician and Basque
among themselves.

Ángela

Es verdad. Y además, es bueno
conocer otros sitios y otras
costumbres. Vamos a ir a San
Sebastián. Allí hay playa, campo,
cultura y también hay buena comida
y buen vino. Y la gente es encantadora.
Podemos alquilar un piso en .
la playa

That's true. And what's more it's
good to get to know other areas
and customs. Let's go to San
Sebastían. There they have the
beach, nature and culture and there's
also good food and good wine.
he people are charming. We can rent
a flat on the beach.

All the adults

Sí, vamos a ir a San Sebastián.

Yes, let's go to San Sebastián.

The story: a tourist in Las Palmas.

Narrator

Un turista en Las Palmas de Gran
Canaria.

A tourist in Las Palmas de
Gran Canaria.

Tourist

Estoy en Las Palmas de Gran Canaria.
Hoy es el día veinte de enero y hace
un día espléndido. Hace calor, pero no
mucho, porque siempre corre un poco de
viento.

I am in Las Palmas de Gran Canaria.
it is a splendid day. It is warm,
but not too warm because there is
always a light breeze.

The story: a man in Valladolid.

Narrator

Un señor en Valladolid.

A man in Valladolid.

Man

Estamos aquí en la ciudad de
Valladolid. Estamos en febrero y
como siempre en esta época hace
un frío que pela. Está nevando y los
niños se lo están pasando bomba.

We are in the city of Valladolid.
It is February and, as always at
this time of year, it is bitterly
cold. It is snowing and the children
are having a lot of fun.

EJERCICIOS

CD3 TOP9 Ejercicio 1:
Utilice el indefinido – Use the "indefinido".

E Ejemplo – Example:

Voz: *¿Dónde estuviste el año pasado?*
Where were you last year?

Usted: *Estuve en la Costa Brava.*
I was on the Costa Brava.

Voz: *Estuve en la Costa Brava.*

Usted: *Estuve en la Costa Brava.*

 Y ahora usted, por favor – and now you:

1. ¿Dónde estuve el año pasado?   Where were you last year?
   Estuve en la Costa Brava.   I was on the Costa Brava.

2. ¿Y Rosa?   And Rosa?
   Estuvo en la Costa Brava.   She was on the Costa Brava.

3. ¿Y tus hermanos?   And your brother/sister?
   Estuvieron en la Costa Brava.   They were on the Costa Brava.

4. ¿Y yo?
   Estuve en la Costa Brava.   I was on the Costa Brava.

5. ¿Y vosotros?
   Estuvisteis en la Costa Brava.   You were on the Costa Brava.

6. ¿Y mis amigas y yo?
   Estuvimos en la Costa Brava.   We were on the Costa Brava.

7. ¿Y ustedes?
   Estuvieron en la Costa Brava.   They were on the Costa Brava.

CD3 TOP10 Ejercicio 2:
Pida lo mismo – ask for the same thing.

 Ejemplo – Example:

Voz:	*Póngame una cerveza.* Bring me a beer.
Usted:	*Póngame a mí otra.* Bring me one too.
Voz:	*Póngame a mí otra.*
Usted:	*Póngame a mí otra.*

 Y ahora usted, por favor – and now you:

1. Póngame una cerveza.   Bring me a beer.
   Póngame a mí otra.   Bring me one too.

2. Quiero un kilo de plátanos.   I would like a kilo of bananas.
   Yo quiero otro.   I would also like a kilo.

201

3. Tráigame una sopa de pescado.   Bring me a fish soup.
   Tráigame a mí otra.   Bring me one as well.

4. Enséñeme los zapatos grises.   Show me the grey shoes.
   Enséñeme a mí otros.   Show me some others/show me
                                   some as well.

5. Quiero comprar una bicicleta.   I want to buy a bicycle.
   Yo quiero comprar otra.   I also want to buy one.

6. Quiero alquilar un piso en la playa. I want to rent a flat on the beach.
   Yo quiero alquilar otro.   I also want to rent one.

7. Necesitamos unos guías alemanes. We need an German tourist guide.
   Nosotros necesitamos otros.   We also need one.

Ejercicio 3:
Responda – reply.

E **Ejemplo – Example:**

Voz: *¿Hace calor en verano?*
          Is it warm in the summer?

Usted: *Sí, hace calor en verano.*
          Yes, it is warm in the summer

Voz: *Sí, hace calor en verano.*

Usted: *Sí, hace calor en verano.*

 Y ahora usted, por favor – and now you:

1. ¿Hace calor en verano?   Is it warm in the summer?
   Sí, hace calor en verano.   Yes, it is warm in the summer.

2. ¿Nieva en primavera?   Does it snow in the spring?
   No, no nieva en primavera.   No, it doesn't snow in the spring.

3. ¿Hace frío en invierno?   Is it cold in the winter?
   Si, hace frío en invierno.   Yes, it is cold in the winter.

4. ¿Hace mucho viento en otoño?   Is it very windy in the autumn?
   Sí, hace mucho viento en otoño.   Yes, it is very windy in the autumn.

5. ¿Hace un tiempo espléndido en   Is the weather in the Canary
   las Islas Canarias?   Islands nice?
   Si, hace un tiempo espléndido en   Yes, the weather in the Canary
   las Islas Canarias.   Islands is nice.

6. ¿Hace mal tiempo en invierno
   en Alemania?
   Sí, hace mal tiempo en invierno
   en Alemania.

   Is the weather in Germany in the
   winter bad?
   Yes, the weather in Germany in the
   winter is bad?

7. ¿Llueve mucho en otoño?
   Sí, llueve mucho en otoño.

   Does it rain a lot in the autumn?
   Yes, it rains a lot in the autumn.

CD3 TOP12 **Ejercicio 4:**
Diga que no lo hagan – **say that they shouldn't do it.**

E Ejemplo – Example:

Voz:	*¡Come!*
	Eat!
Usted:	*¡No comas!*
	Don't eat!
Voz:	*¡No comas!*
Usted:	*¡No comas!*

1.

2.

3.

Y ahora usted, por favor – and now you:

1. ¡Come!   Eat!
   ¡No comas!   Don't eat!

2. ¡Trabaja!   Work!
   ¡No trabajes! Don't work

3. ¡Bebe!   Drink!
   ¡No bebas!   Don't drink!

4. ¡Habla!   Speak!
   ¡No hables!   Don't speak!

5. ¡Pasad!   Come in/go in!
   ¡No paséis!   Don't come in/go in!

6. ¡Escribid!   Write!
   ¡No escribáis! Don't write!

7. ¡Pagad!   Pay!
   ¡No paguéis! Don't pay!

GRAMÁTICA

Expressions of Time

When discussing the "imperfecto" we saw that the use of Spanish tenses is complex and similar to English. The various Spanish tenses are not only used to indicate when something happened but also to say whether the action occured over a shorter or longer period of time, and whether it happened once or on repeated occasions. This sensitivity to time in Spanish is also reflected in the way in which other expressions of time are used:

durante el mes de agosto	in August (literally: during the month of August)

Durante – during, is used to express a period of time and not just a single point in time. When using ***durante*** a period of time is also required: in this case ***el mes*** – the month.

Here are some other expressions of time:

durante el año de mil novecientos noventa y nueve	in 1999
durante la semana de vacaciones	during the holidays (weeks of the holiday)
durante la hora de la cena	during dinner
durante los meses de verano	in the summer months
durante el día de año nuevo	on New Year's Day

Supplementary Exercise 1
Form expressions of time similar to the example.

Example: noviembre; durante el mes de noviembre
1. noviembre;
2. mil novecientos noventa y nueve;
3. navidad;
4. invierno.

el año pasado	last year
el año anterior	the year before that (literally: the previous year)
el año que viene	next year (literally: the year which comes)

Examples:

El año pasado estuvimos en la Costa del Sol y el año anterior en la Costa Brava.	Last year we were on the Costa del Sol and the year before that we were on the Costa Brava.
La semana pasada estuve en España y la semana anterior en Argentina.	Last week I was in Spain and the week before I was in Argentina.
El mes pasado estuvieron en casa de María y el mes anterior en la casa de Matilde.	Last month we were at Maria's house and the month before at Mathilde's house.
Este año voy al instituto y el año que viene voy a la universidad.	This year I am going to sixth-form college and next year I will be going to university.
todo el día	all day long (for the whole day)
toda la noche	all night long
todo el año	all year long
toda la vida	for all of (his, her, my ...) life

The compound ***de toda la vida*** is often used to mean "always"

Example:

Se hace así de toda la vida.	It's always been done that way.

Supplementary Exercise 2

Reply to the following questions using the compounds todo el día , todo la noche etc.

Example: ¿Has dormido esta noche? Sí, he dormido toda la noche.
1. ¿Has dormido esta noche?
2. ¿Has trabajado hoy?
3. ¿Has tenido trabajo este año?
4. ¿Has leído hoy?

The "Indefinido"

In the last lesson we met one of the two simple past forms of *estar*, namely the "imperfecto". In this lesson we will look at the corresponding forms of the second simple past form – the "indefinido". In the "indefinido" the action is something which has run its course and was completed in the past. In the "imperfecto" the action started in the past and continued on repeated occasions.
Whilst the "imperfecto" is used to describe how something was, the "indefinido" is used to report on the action, i.e. what happened. We would like to emphasise once again that the differences between the "imperfecto" and the "indefinido" can't be learnt overnight. Apart from this, using the incorrect form hardly ever causes problems in making oneself understood.

Use of the Past Tenses:

A. Reporting an action: *What happened?*

(a) When related to the present: PERFECTO

(b) If there is no link to the present: INDEFINIDO

B. Description: *How was something?*

habitual actions
things and people   IMPERFECTO
situations or the background to an action

Example:

El año pasado estuvimos en la Costa del Sol y el año anterior en la Costa Brava.	Last year we were on the Costa de Sol and the year before on the Costa Brava.

		ESTAR (indefinido)
	1. Pers.	*estuve*
Singular	2. Pers.	*estuviste*
	3. Pers.	*estuvo*
	1. Pers.	*estuvimos*
Plural	2. Pers.	*estuvisteis*
	3. Pers.	*estuvieron*

The Preposition *de* + Article

de + *el* are compounded to form *del*
 la familia del hermano — the family of the brother
 (the brother's family)

Examples:
 la familia del hermano de don José — the family of Don José's brother
 la familia del abuelo — the grandfather's family

but:
 la familia de la madre — the mother's family
 la familia de los padres — the parents' family
 la familia de las hermanas — the family of the brothers and sisters

Otro/otra

Otro changes its ending depending on number and gender:
 otro viaje — another journey
 otros países — other countries
 otra casa — another house
 otras ciudades — other cities

Example:
 Este año quiero ver otras partes de España. — This year I would like to see other parts of Spain.

The word *otro* does not only mean "another" or "other", but also "(yet) another" (in the singular) or "more" (in the plural).

Example:

Quiero otra cerveza.	I want another beer.
Tráigame otro café.	Bring me another coffee.

Otro can also be used on its own.

Examples:

Póngame una cerveza.	Bring me a beer.
Y a mí otra.	(Bring) me one too.
Quiero un bocadillo de queso.	I would like a cheese roll.
Yo quiero otro.	I would also like one.
No me gustan estos pantalones.	I don't like these trousers.
Enséñeme otros.	Show me another pair.
No me gustan estas camisas.	I don't like these shirts.
Prefiero otras.	I would prefer some others.

Con + Personal Pronoun

The forms "with me" and "with you" are always:

> **conmigo**
> **contigo**

Example:

Estoy de acuerdo contigo.	I agree with you.
Él está de acuerdo conmigo.	He agrees with me.

In the third person *consigo/a* is used (in the singular) and *con ellos/as mismos/as* (in the plural), but only if the form is used reflexively. In these cases the word *mismo/a/os/as* (self) is often added:

consigo mismo	with himself
	(for a masculine subject in the singular)
consigo misma	with herself
	(for a feminine subject in the singular)
con ellos mismos	with themselves
	(for a masculine or mixed gender subject in the plural)
con ellas mismas	with themselves
	(for a feminine subject in the plural)

Example:

Pepe habla consigo mismo.	Pepe talks to (lit: with) himself.
María habla consigo misma.	Maria talks to (lit: with) herself.
Ellos hablan con ellos mismos.	They talk to (lit: with) themselves.
Ellas hablan con ellas mismas.	They talk to (lit: with) themselves. (woman or girls)

For non-reflexive forms in the third person, i.e. when the subject and object are different people the following forms are used:

> *con él*
> *con ella*
> *con usted*

Examples:

Estamos de acuerdo con él.	We agree with him.
Estamos de acuerdo con ella.	We agree with her.
Estamos de acuerdo con usted.	We agree with you.

In the plural all of the forms are regular:

> *con nosotros*
> *con vosotros*
> *con ellos; con ellas; con ustedes*

Examples:

Tú estás de acuerdo con él.	You agree with him.
Estoy de acuerdo con ellos.	I agree with them.
Ellos están de acuerdo con nosotros.	They agree with us.

Supplementary Exercise 3
Use the personal pronoun with *con*. Reply to the question "Who are you speaking to?" by translating the English forms into Spanish.

Example: ¿Con quién estás hablando? (to him); Estoy hablando con él.
¿Con quién estás hablando?
1. to him;
2. to you (singular);
3. to you (plural);
4. to myself.

The weather

Hace calor.	It is warm.
Hace mucho calor.	It is hot.

Other expressions to do with the weather which you should know:

Hace un día espléndido.	It is a wonderful/splendid day.
Luce el sol.	The sun is shining.
Está nublado.	It is cloudy.
Hace frío.	It is cold.
Hace un frío que pela.	It is bitterly cold. (literally: it is so cold that the skin peels.)
Hace viento.	It is windy.
Corre un poco de viento.	There is a light breeze. (literally: a little wind is running.)
Hace mucho viento.	It is stormy.
Llueve.	It rains.
Está lloviendo.	It is raining.
Llueve a cántaros.	It is pouring. (literally: it's raining jugs [bucket])
Nieva.	It snows.
Está nevando.	It is snowing.
Hay tormenta.	There's a storm.
¡terremoto!	Earthquake!

Tanto – tantísimo

Hace mucho calor.	It's hot.
Hace tanto calor.	It's so hot.

Examples:

En el sur hace mucho calor.	In the south it is very hot.
En el norte no hace tanto calor.	In the north it is not so hot.

The adjective *tanto* can, depending on context, also be translated by "so much", "so long" (for time phrases) or by "such":

tanto dinero	so much money
tanta sed	so thirsty (lit: such a thirst)
tanto tiempo	such a long time

Supplementary Exercise 4a
Make the following statements more acute by using the adjective *tanto*.

Example: Tengo trabajo. ¡Tengo tanto trabajo!
1. Tengo trabajo.
2. Hace frío.
3. Hace viento.
4. Jaime tiene dinero.

If you want to make the statement even more acute you can use *tantísimo* instead *tanto*:

Example:
¡Tengo tantísimo frío!   I am so terribly cold!

Supplementary Exercise 4b
Now use *tantísimo*.

Example: Anita tiene sueño. Anita tiene tantísimo sueño.
1. Anita tiene sueño.
2. Tengo sed.
3. Tenemos calor.
4. Rita tiene amigos.

Tanto can also be used as an adverb, i.e. it can be used with a verb. In this case the translation is "so (very) much" or "such a long time". *Tanto* can also be used to intensify the meaning of **mucho**. This usage is also made clear by stressing the word:

Example:

Llueve mucho.	It rains a lot.
¡Llueve tanto!	It rains so (very) much!

Here as well *tanto* can be intensified through the use of *tantísimo*:

¡Llueve tantísimo!	There's such an awful lot of rain!

Supplementary Exercise 4c
Make the following statements even more acute.

Example: Mónica duerme. ¡Mónica duerme tanto!
1. Mónica duerme.
2. Enrique trabaja.
3. Estamos comiendo.
4. Los niños estudian.

When used in conjunction with another adverb or adjective,
the short form *tan* is used instead of *tanto*:

No comas tan rápido.	Don't eat so quickly.
No bebas el café tan caliente.	Don't drink the coffee while it's so hot.

The Verb *saber*

The verb ***saber*** (to know/to be able to) is conjugated irregularly. In the present tense it is only irregular, though, in the first person singular.

		SABER (Present)
	1. Pers.	*sé*
Singular	2. Pers.	*sabes*
	3. Pers.	*sabe*
	1. Pers.	*sabemos*
Plural	2. Pers.	*sabéis*
	3. Pers.	*saben*

Sé hablar inglés.	I can speak English (literally: I know how to speak English.)
Sé conducir.	I can drive.
Sé nadar.	I can swim.

BUT

Manuel se casa. – Lo sé.	Manuel is getting married. – I know (that).
Sé que Manuel se casa.	I know that Manuel is getting married.

Supplementary Exercise 5

In the following exercise you will be asked if you already know about a particular piece of news. Answer the question in the affirmative. Note whether the question is worded in the singular or the plural.

Example: ¿Sabéis que Carmen se casa? – Sí, lo sabemos.
1. ¿Sabéis que Carmen se casa?
2. ¿Sabes que me voy a Alemania?
3. ¿Sabe usted que don Enrique es médico?
4. ¿Saben ustedes dónde está la salida?

The "subjuntivo"

Niños, no seáis tontos.	Children, don't be silly.

In lesson VII we saw how the imperative was formed. You will remember:

Rellene el impreso.	Fill out the form.
Escriba el número de su cuenta.	Enter your account number.

If an order or command is expressed in a negative form, i.e. using a negation, the subjunctive (*el subjuntivo*) is used instead of the imperative form. The subjunctive in Spanish is used differently to the way it is used in other languages you might know, such as German. The negated request or command is only one of a number of uses. The present subjunctive of the verb *ser* is formed as follows:

			SER (Present subjunctive)
		1. Pers.	*sea*
Singular		2. Pers.	*seas*
		3. Pers.	*sea*
		1. Pers.	*seamos*
Plural		2. Pers.	*seáis*
		3. Pers.	*sean*

Example:

¡Anda, Miguel, no seas tonto!	Come on Miguel, don't be silly.
¡Venga, Doña Rosa,	Come on Doña Rosa, don't be silly.
no sea usted tonta!	Don't be silly.
¡Venid, no seáis tontos!	Come on, don't be silly.
	(second person plural)

Present Subjunctive of Regular Verbs Ending in *-ar, -er* und *-ir*

		TOMAR	COMER	VIVIR
Singular	1. Pers.	tome	coma	viva
	2. Pers.	tomes	comas	vivas
	3. Pers.	tome	coma	viva
Plural	1. Pers.	tomemos	comamos	vivamos
	2. Pers.	toméis	comáis	viváis
	3. Pers.	tomen	coman	vivan

You will notice that the endings in the subjunctive only differ from the present indicative in the vowel that is used. And in the subjunctive, verbs are even more regular since verbs ending in *–ar* always have an **e** in their ending and verbs ending in *–er* and *–ir* always have an **a**.
So forming the subjunctive isn't really difficult. It is the use of the subjunctive which is more difficult. But we won't discuss this topic until later.

Aquí – ahí – allí

The Spanish adverbs of place *aquí - ahí - allí* differ from the English "here" and "there" in that a distinction is made between three different degrees of proximity:

aquí	here
ahí	there (a little further away)
allí	there (a lot further away)

Example:

Vamos a ir a San Sebastián.
Allí hay playa, campo y cultura.

Let's go to San Sebastián.
(Over) there, there are beaches, nature and culture.

The Adjectives *bueno* and *malo*

In contrast to most adjectives, **bueno** and **malo** usually precede the noun.
Also, in the masculine singular the final -o disappears:

Examples:
> *la buena comida*
> *la mala comida*
> *el buen vino*
> *el mal vino*
> *las buenas amigas*
> *las malas amigas*
> *los buenos hoteles*
> *los malos hoteles*

> *Hay buena comida y buen vino.*   There is good food and good wine.

Vocabulary

La reunión

la reunión familiar the family get together / family reunion / meeting

Other common types of "meeting":
> *la reunión de trabajo*   meeting at work
> *la reunión de negocios*   business meeting
> *la reunión política*   political meeting/rally
> *la reunión de amigos*   reunion or get together of a group
>   friends

Pasárselo bomba

The reflexive form ***pasárselo bomba*** (to have a lot of fun) is used as follows:
> *Me lo paso bomba.*   I have a lot of fun.
> *Te lo pasas bomba.*   You have a lot of fun.
> *Se lo pasa bomba.*   He/she has a lot of fun.
> etc.

I speak Spanish

There are two different ways of saying that you can speak a language:
1. *Hablo español.*   I speak Spanish.
2. *Sé hablar español.*   I know how to speak Spanish.

The impersonal form *se **habla**,* literally translated, means "one speaks". This form could be translated in English by a passive construction "Spanish is spoken"

Example:
Aquí se habla inglés.   English is spoken here.

Passive constructions are not as common in Spanish as they are in English. If you want to make an impersonal or general statement which is generally applicable, i.e. a statement without a subject, then you either use the impersonal *se* or formulate the statement in the plural leaving out the subject.
Examples:
En España se habla español   OR   *En España hablan español.*
En España se baila flamenco   OR   *En España bailan flamenco.*
En España se come paella   OR   *En España comen paella.*

Entre ellos

Entre ellos – amongst themselves (when referring to males or masculine objects or a mixed group);
entre ellas - amongst themselves (when only referring to females or feminine objects).

Example:
El gallego o el vasco, lo hablan   Gallician or Basque, they only speak
sólo entre ellos.   that amongst themselves.

Es bueno hacer algo
Es bueno hacer algo   It is good to get to know other areas
     and other customs.

Example:
Es bueno conocer otros sitios y   It is good to get to know other areas
otras costumbres.   and other customs.

Other examples:

Es bueno hablar muchos idiomas.	It is good to speak a lot of languages.
Es bueno dormir ocho horas.	It is good to sleep for 8 hours.
Es bueno comer pescado.	It is good (healthy) to eat fish.
No es bueno beber mucha cerveza.	It isn't good to drink lots of beer.
No es bueno comer mucha carne.	It isn't good to eat lots of meat.
No es bueno trabajar demasiado.	It isn't good to work too much.

La gente

The collective term *la gente* is used in Spanish in the singular. Accordingly, the accompanying verb also takes the singular form:

Examples:

La gente es encantadora.	The people are charming.
La gente habla mucho.	People speak a lot.
La gente es muy mala.	People are very bad.

Alquilar

The word *alquilar* means "to rent out" as well „to rent (from)".

Alquilo un piso en la playa.	(a) I rent a flat at the beach.
	(b) I rent out a flat at the beach.

The meaning is usually clear from the context.

Podemos alquilar un piso en la playa.	We can rent a flat on the beach.

Information about the Country

Four different languages are spoken in Spain as well as various dialects:

1. *El castellano*, is the official language of Spain. This language was orginally spoken in Castille (*Castilla*). Today, *Castellano* is spoken all over Spain and in the Spanish-speaking countries of Latin America. Variations to the language in the individual countries are relatively insignificant and the main differences are in vocabulary.
Standard Spanish, *castellano*, is spoken today by some 300 million people around the world and is thus the most widely spoken of the Romance languages.

2. *El catalán*, Catalan. This language is spoken in Catalonia (*Cataluña*) and is the offical language there alongside *castellano*. Despite being suppressed for decades by the Franco dictatorship, the language is flourishing today. Valencian and Mallorcan are variants of Catalan. Both *el castellano* and *el catalán* are Romance languages. For this reason, both languages have a lot in common.

3. *El vasco*, Basque. This language has been spoken with varying degrees of regularity in the Basque Country (*el País Vasco*). Basque is the official language there together with *castellano*. After seeing a marked decline during the Franco dictatorship, great efforts are being made today to revitalise the language. Basque is not an Indo-Germanic language and is not related to any European language.

4. *El gallego*, Gallician, is the language spoken in Gallicia where it is also the official language. Gallician is related to Portuguese – in fact Portuguese forms the foundation of the language. Gallician is also a Romance

Supplementary Exercise 6
Read the following text.

En España se hablan cuatro idiomas, el castellano, el catalán, el vasco y el gallego. El castellano se habla en toda España y en Hispanoamérica. En Cataluña se habla castellano y catalán. El catalán lo hablan los catalanes sólo entre ellos. En el País Vasco se habla castellano y vasco. El vasco lo hablan los vascos entre ellos. En Galicia se habla castellano y gallego. También el gallego lo hablan los gallegos sólo entre ellos.

Solutions to the Supplementary Exercises

Supplementary Exercise 1

1. Sí, he dormido toda la noche.
2. Sí, he trabajado todo el día.
3. Sí, he tenido trabajo todo el año.
4. Sí, he leído todo el día.

Supplementary Exercise 2

1. durante el mes de noviembre;
2. durante el año mil novecientos noventa y nueve;
3. durante el día de navidad;
4. durante los meses de invierno.

Supplementary Exercise 3

1. Estoy hablando con él.
2. Estoy hablando contigo.
3. Estoy hablando con vosotros.
4. Estoy hablando conmigo mismo.

Supplementary Exercise 4a

1. ¡Tengo tanto trabajo!
2. ¡Hace tanto frío!
3. ¡Hace tanto viento!
4. ¡Jaime tiene tanto dinero!

Supplementary Exercise 4b

1. ¡Anita tiene tantísimo sueño!
2. ¡Tengo tantísima sed!
3. ¡Tenemos tantísimo calor!
4. ¡Rita tiene tantísimos amigos!

Supplementary Exercise 4c

1. ¡Mónica duerme tanto!
2. ¡Enrique trabaja tanto!
3. ¡Estamos comiendo tanto!
4. ¡Los niños estudian tanto!

Supplementary Exercise 5

1. Sí, lo sabemos.
2. Sí, lo sé.
3. Sí, lo sé.
4. Sí, lo sabemos.

Supplementary Exercise 6

In Spain four languages are spoken, Spanish, Catalan, Basque and Gallician. Spanish is spoken everywhere in Spain and in Hispano America. In Catalonia, Spanish and Catalan are spoken. The Catalans only speak Catalan amongst themselves. In the Basque Country Spanish and Basque are spoken. Basque is only spoken by the Basque amongst themselves. In Gallicia Spanish and Gallician are spoken. Gallician is also only spoken by the Gallicians amongst themselves.

In this lesson you will learn how to:

- describe a flat
- refer to household items
- talk about sport

CD3 Remember the following expressions and phrases:
TOP13

Los estábamos esperando.	We have been expecting you.
Seguro que están cansados del viaje.	You must be tired from the journey.
Pueden descansar tranquilamente.	You can recover in peace and quiet.
muy amable	That's very kind of you
¿Qué tal el viaje?	How was the journey?
el cuarto de baño	the bathroom
La cocina está totalmente equipada.	The kitchen is fully equipped.
detrás de la puerta	behind the door
No funciona la luz.	The light doesn't work.
el interruptor de la luz	the light switch
al lado de la puerta	next to the door
¿Has visto?	Can you see?
¿Qué, te gusta?	So, do you like it?
Hombre, no está mal.	Mmm!, it's not bad.
en frente de la cocina	opposite the kitchen
Está todo muy bien.	Everything is very good.
Oye, ¿qué hacemos mañana?	Listen, what are we going to do tomorrow?
No sé.	I don't know.

Me gustaría hacer algo de deporte.	I would like to do a little sport
Hay muchas posibilidades.	There are lots of possibilities.
Todo el mundo juega a algo.	Everyone plays something.
Me gustaría hacer algo diferente.	I would like to do something different
algo que no haya hecho nunca	something that I haven't done before
un campo de golf	a golf course
una pista de tenis	a tennis court
Mañana me informaré.	Tomorrow I will enquire (inform myself).
Me basta con un poco de natación.	A little swimming is enough for me.
un paseo por la playa	a walk on the beach
Te acompaño.	I'll accompany you.
dar una vuelta en bicicleta	to ride around by bike
estupendo	great!
tomar el sol	to sunbathe
Hay que ver.	Oh, really!

CD3 TOP14 A: DIÁLOGOS

The story: Both families arrive at the rented holiday flat. The landlady tells her guests where everything is.

Ángela

Buenas tardes, somos la familia Delgado, los que hemos alquilado

Good day, we are the Delgado family who have rented the flat.

Angustias

Ah, muy bien, bienvenidos, pasen, por favor. Los estábamos esperando. Seguro que están cansados del viaje. Si quieren les enseño rápidamente el piso y ya pueden descansar tranquilamente. ¿Qué tal el viaje?

Oh, how nice, welcome. Please come in. We have been expecting you. You must be tired from the journey. If you want, I'll quickly show you around the flat and then you can recover in peace and quiet. How was the journey?

Ángela

Muy bien, gracias, muy amable.

Very good thank you, nice of you to ask.

Angustias

Bueno, pues, aquí en la entrada tienen un pequeño recibidor. A la derecha está el cuarto de baño con su ducha, su bañera y un lavabo.

Now then, here at the entrance you have a small hallway. To the right is the bathroom with shower, bath and wash basin.

Jesús

Y, ¿dónde está el water?

And where is the loo?

Angustias

El inodoro se encuentra en otro servicio aparte, al lado del cuarto de baño. Pasen, por favor. Aquí tenemos uno de los dormitorios con dos camas individuales, dos mesitas de noche y un armario.

The toilet is in a separate room next to the bathroom. Come on through please. Here we have one of the bedrooms with two single beds, two bed-side tables and a wardrobe.

Jesús

¡No hay espejo!

There's no mirror here!

Angustias

Sí, hay uno, está dentro del armario.
Las dos habitaciones siguientes
también son dormitorios, uno de
matrimonio y otro individual.
Aquí a la izquierda está la cocina.
Está totalmente equipada, con su
hornilla de gas, su fregadero, su mesa
con las sillas, sus platos, vasos y copas,
sus cubiertos, ollas y sartenes. Y aquí
al fondo está el lavavajillas y la lavadora.
Detrás de esa puerta hay una despensa.

Yes, there's one in the wardrobe.
The next two rooms are also bedrooms, one with a double bed and
a single room. Here on to the left
is the kitchen. It is fully equipped
with a gas cooker, sink, dining
table, plates, glasses, cutlery, pots
and pans. And here at the back is
the dishwasher. Behind this door
there's a larder.

Jesús

Mamá, ¡no funciona la luz!

Mummy, the light doesn't work!

Angustias

No, hijo mío, ésste no es el interruptor
de la luz de la cocina,ésste es el de la
terraza. El interruptor de la cocina
está aquí, al lado de la puerta.

No, my child, that isn't the light
switch for the kitchen, that's the one
for the terrace. The light switch
for the kitchen is here next to
the door.

Jesús

Sí, es verdad, funciona.

Yes, that's right, it works.

Angustias

¿Has visto? y ¿qué, te gusta el piso?

Can you see? So do you like
the flat?

Jesús

Hombre, no está mal, pero no hay
televisión.

Mmm!, it's not bad but there
isn't a television.

Angustias

Sí, también hay televisión. Está en el
salón, en frente de la cocina. Pasen.
Aquí tienen un sofá y dos butacas y
una mesa baja, una mesa grande para
comer y una estantería.

Yes, there's also a television.
It's in the living room opposite
the kitchen. Come on through.
Here you have a sofa and two
armchairs, a low table (coffee
table), a large dining table and
some shelves.

Ángela

Muy bien, está todo muy bien.

Very good, everything is very nice.

The story: The family plan what they are going to do on the first day of the holiday.

Ángela

Oye, ¿qué hacemos mañana? | Listen, what are we going to do tomorrow?

José

No sé. A mí me gustaría hacer algo de deporte. Seguro que aquí hay muchas posibilidades. | I don't know. I would like to do a little sport. There are certainly a lot of possibilities here.

Jesús

Sí, claro, he visto que en la playa todo el mundo juega a algo, voléibol, fútbol, badminton e incluso baloncesto. | Yes, sure, I've (just) seen that everyone was playing something on the on the beach, volleyball, football, badminton and even basketball.

Maira

Sí, y también hay muchos que hacen windsurfing, vela, esquí acuático y submarinismo. | Yes and a lot of people are also windsurfing, sailing, waterskiing and diving.

José

No, a mi me gustaría hacer algo diferente, algún deporte que no haya hecho nunca, tenis o golf. Me parece que aquí cerca hay un gran campo de golf y pistas de tenis hay en frente de la casa. Mañana me informaré. | No, I would rather do something else, some sort of sport that I haven't done before. Tennis or golf. I think there's a large golf course nearby and there are tennis courts directly opposite the house. Tomorrow I will inform myself.

Ángela

Pues a mí me basta con un poco de natación y algún que otro paseo por la playa. | For me a little swimming and some walks along the beach would be enough.

Jesus

Yo te acompaño. Y por la tarde podemos dar una vuelta en bicicleta. | I'll accompany you. And in the afternoons we can do a bike tour.

Ángela

¡Estupendo! | Great!

Maira

Yo no quiero hacer ningún deporte.
Mi deporte será dormir mucho y tomar el sol.

I don't want to do any sport at all.
My sport is lots of sleeping and sunbathing.

Ángela

Hay que ver.

Well really!

B: EJERCICIOS

Ejercicio 1:

¿Dónde están las cosas normalmente? – Where can the following items normally be found?

E Ejemplo – Example:

Voz: *¿Dónde están las camas?*
        Where are the beds?

Usted: *Las camas están en el dormitorio.*
        The beds are in the bedroom.

Voz: *Las camas están en el dormitorio.*

Usted: *Las camas están en el dormitorio.*

Y ahora usted, por favor – and now you:

1. ¿Dónde están las camas?
   Las camas están en el dormitorio.

   Where are the beds?
   The beds are in the bedroom.

2. ¿Dónde está la hornilla?
   La hornilla está en la cocina.

   Where is the cooker?
   The cooker is in the kitchen.

3. ¿Dónde está la ducha?
   La ducha está en el cuarto de baño.

   Where is the shower?
   The shower is in the bathroom.

4. ¿Dónde está la televisión?
   La televisión está en el salón.

   Where is the television?
   The television is in the living room.

5. ¿Dónde están las mesitas de noche?
   Las mesitas de noche están en el
   dormitorio.

   Where are the bed-side tables?
   The bed-side tables are in the
   bedroom.

6. ¿Dónde están las butacas y el sofá?

   Las butacas y el sofá están en el salón.

   Where are the armchairs and
   the sofa?
   The armchairs and the sofa are in
   the living room.

7. ¿Dónde está el frigorífico?
   El frigorífico está en la cocina.

   Where is the refrigerator?
   The refrigerator is in the kitchen.

CD3 Ejercicio 2:
TOP16

Diga que lo haga bien – Say that he should do it properly.

E **Ejemplo – Example:**

Voz: *Paquito, no pongas los pies encima de la mesa.*
          Paquito, don't put your feet on the table.

Usted: *Ponlos debajo de la mesa.*
          Put them under the table.

Voz: *Ponlos debajo de la mesa.*

Usted: *Ponlos debajo de la mesa.*

 Y ahora usted, por favor – and now you:

1. Paquito, no pongas los pies encima   Paquito, don't put your feet
   de la mesa.   on the table.
   Ponlos debajo de la mesa.   Put them under the table.

2. No pongas las flores dentro del   Don't put the flowers in the
   armario.   cupboard.
   Ponlas encima del armario.   Put them on top of the cupboard.

3. No pongas las cucharas delante   Don't put the spoon in front
   de los platos.   of the plate.
   Ponlas al lado de los platos.   Put it next to the plate.

4. No pongas la cerveza encima de   Don't put the beer on top of the
   frigorífico.   refrigerator.
   Ponla dentro del frigorífico.   Put it in the refrigerator.

5. No pongas las manos en el plato.
   Ponlas al lado del plato.

Don't put your hands in
the bowl.
Put them next to the bowl.

6. No dejes al gato encima de la mesa.
   Déjalo debajo de la mesa.

Don't let the cat (get) on the table.
Put it under the table.

7. No te sientes debajo de la silla.
   Siéntate encima de la silla.

Don't sit underneath the chair.
Sit on the chair.

Ejercicio 3:

Diga qué deporte practica – Say what kind of sport the people named do.

(E) **Ejemplo – Example:**

Voz: *Arantxa Sánchez*

Usted: *Arantxa Sánchez juega al tenis.*
          Arantxa Sánchez plays tennis.

Voz: *Arantxa Sánchez juega al tenis.*

Usted: *Arantxa Sánchez juega al tenis.*

Y ahora usted, por favor – and now you:

1. Arantxa Sánchez
   Arantxa Sánchez juega al tenis.   Arantxa Sánchez plays tennis.

2. Ronaldo
   Ronaldo juega al fútbol.   Ronaldo plays football.

3. Michael Jordan
   Michael Jordan juega al baloncesto.   Michael Jordan plays basketball.

4. Juri Kasparov
   Juri Kasparov juega al ajedrez.   Juri Kasparov plays chess.

5. Jan Ullrich
   Jan Ullrich practica el ciclismo.   Jan Ullrich cycles.

6. Severiano Ballesteros
   Severiano Ballesteros juega al golf.   Severiano Ballesteros plays golf.

7. Reinhold Messner
   Reinhold Messner practica   Reinhold Messner is a mountain
   el alpinismo.   climber. (literally: practices
                                            "Alpinism")

CD3 Ejercicio 4:
TOP18

Responda – reply.

E **Ejemplo – Example:**

Voz: *¿Hay playas en San Sebastián?*
Are there beaches in San Sebastián?

Usted: *Sí, hay playas en San Sebastián.*
Yes, there are beaches in San Sebastián.

Voz: *Sí, hay playas en San Sebastián.*

Usted: *Sí, hay playas en San Sebastián.*

 Y ahora usted, por favor – and now you:

1. ¿Hay playas en San Sebastián?
   Sí, hay playas en San Sebastián.

   Are there beaches in San Sebastián?
   Yes, there are beaches in San Sebastián.

2. ¿Se pueden alquilar pisos en San Sebastián?
   Sí, se pueden alquilar pisos en San Sebastián.

   Can you rent flats in San Sebastián?
   Yes, you can rent flats in San Sebastián.

3. ¿Juega la gente al voléibol en la playa?
   Sí, la gente juega al voléibol en la playa.

   Do people play volleyball on the beach?
   Yes, people play volleyball on the beach.

4. ¿Se puede jugar al golf en la playa?
No, no se puede jugar al golf en la playa.

Can you play golf on the beach?
No, you can't play golf on the beach.

5. Los vascos, ¿saben hablar español?
Si, los vascos saben hablar español.

Can the Basques speak Spanish?
Yes, the Basques can speak Spanish.

6. ¿Llueve mucho en el País Vasco?

Sí, llueve mucho en el País Vasco.

Does it rain a lot in the Basque Country?
Yes, it rains a lot in the Basque Country.

7. ¿Hay buena comida y buen vino en el País Vasco?
Sí, hay buena comida y buen vino en el País Vasco.

Is there good food and good wine in the Basque country?
Yes, there is good food and good wine in the Basque country.

GRAMÁTICA

The Prepositions

Prepositions which will help you to say where something is:

al lado de – next to

Example:

El inodoro se encuentra en otro servicio aparte, al lado del cuarto de baño.	The toilet is in a separate room next to the bathroom.

dentro de – in (you can also say *en*). The preposition en can also have another meaning though. So use dentro de when you want to make it quite clear that you mean "in a closed space".

Example:

Sí, hay un espejo, está dentro del armario.	Yes, there's a mirror, it's in the cupboard.

detrás de – behind

Example:

Detrás de esa puerta hay una despensa.	Behind this door is a larder.

Some other important prepositions:

delante de	in front of
debajo de	under
encima de	above and on top of
en el centro	in the middle

Supplementary Exercise 1

Look at the picture and say where the items or people named are located.

Example: la mesa; La mesa está en el centro de la habitación.

1. la mesa;
2. los platos;
3. el niño;
4. el hombre;
5. el frigorífico;
6. la pelota;
7. los vasos.

Su

It is likely you will have noticed that Doña Angustias used the possessive pronoun *su* a lot:

> *Aquí a la izquierda está la cocina.*   Here to the left is the kitchen.
> *Está totalmente equipada, con*   It is fully equipped with a gas cooker,
> *su hornilla de gas, su fregadero,*   sink, dining table and chairs,
> *su mesa con las sillas, sus platos,*   plates, glasses, cutlery,
> *vasos y copas, sus cubiertos,*   pots and pans.
> *ollas y sartenes.*

This use of the possessive pronoun is very common in Spanish. It is used to express the fact that something belongs together – in this case that something is as is it should be (the kitchen with its gas cooker): la cocina con su hornilla de gas, etc.

The Verb *jugar*

The verb *jugar* (to play) modifies its root vowel in the singular and the third person plural:

		JUGAR (Present)
	1. Pers.	*juego*
Singular	2. Pers.	*juegas*
	3. Pers.	*juega*
	1. Pers.	*jugamos*
Plural	2. Pers.	*jugáis*
	3. Pers.	*juegan*

To play a game is always conveyed by the phrase jugar *a* algo. You must remember here that a + el is compounded to form *al* and that a + la remains *a la*:

jugar al fútbol	to play football
jugar al baloncesto	to play basketball
jugar al tenis	to play tennis
jugar al badminton	to play badminton
jugar al ajedrez	to plays chess
jugar al dominó	to play dominoes
jugar al monopoli	to play Monopoly
jugar a la pelota	to play ball
jugar a las cartas	to play cards

Vocabulary

Salón – salita – comedor – cuarto de estar

Many Spanish flats have a room called *la salita* or *cuarto de estar* where the family eats and spends its time together as well as the *salón* which is used for more formal occasions. In many places this room is known as *el comedor* (dining room).

Terraza – balcón

la terraza	the large balcony, terrace or roof terrace
el balcón	the balcony

Wáter – inodoro – servicio

El wáter – the toilet (the toilet bowl); the term wáter comes from the English "water closet". The word wáter is relatively popular and is comparable to the English word "loo".
El inodoro – the toilet (the toilet bowl); this is the more refined term.
El servicio – is the standard term for toilet.

Example:

¿Dónde están los servicios?	Where are the toilets?

La hornilla

La hornilla de gas	the gas cooker
La hornilla eléctrica	the electric cooker (electric cookers are still relatively seldom in Spain)

El vaso – la copa

In contrast to English, a distinction is made in Spanish between *vaso* and *copa*:

el vaso	the glass (for water)
la copa	the glass (with a stem for wine, beer etc.)

The Most Important Items of Cutlery

la cuchara	the spoon
el tenedor	the fork
el cuchillo	the knife

Ir en bicicleta

Ir en bicicleta to ride a bicycle i.e. as a mode of transport.
Correr en bicicleta is used when you mean that you cycle as a sport.
Dar una vuelta en bicicleta means "to ride around on a bicycle" or "to go on a little cycle tour".

La pelota – el balón

The word *pelota* is used to mean a ball in general. For football the word *el balón* is used.

Solutions to the Supplementary Exercises

Supplementary Exercise 1

1. La mesa está en el centro de la habitación.
2. Los platos están encima de la mesa.
3. El niño está debajo de la mesa.
4. El hombre está delante del fregadero.
5. El frigorífico está al lado del fregadero.
6. La pelota está detrás del niño.
7. Los vasos están dentro del armario.

In this lesson you will learn how to:

- talk about events in the past
- talk about actions which take place in the future

CD3
TOP19 Remember the following expressions and phrases:

Llegaron a Ingleterra hace veinticinco años.	The came to the UK 25 years ago.
Son auténticos ingleses.	They are British citizens.
Ni siquiera saben hablar español.	They can't even speak Spanish
sin embargo	nevertheless
Tienen visita.	They have visitors.
Están hablando de su vida.	They are talking about their life.
una fábrica de coches	a car factory
cuando tuvimos los niños	when we had the children
Dejó de trabajar.	He/she stopped working.
Volvía a casa sobre las cuatro.	I always returned home at around six o'clock
No me digas.	You're not telling me....
dime	Tell me...
¿Qué hacen ahora?	What are they doing now?
su propia familia	his/her own family
¿No quieren volver a España?	Don't they want to return to Spain?
qué va	No!

Si casi no saben hablar español.	They can speak hardly any Spanish.
Están muy bien.	They are doing very well.
¿Qué van a tomar?	What are you going to have?
unas tapas de jamón serrano	a few raw ham hors d'oeuvres
Tráiganos una botella de agua	Bring a bottle of water.
una paella valenciana	a Valencian paella
una sopa de pollo	a chicken soup
salmón al horno	fried salmon
solomillo a la plancha	grilled fillet steak
¿Quieren pedir algo más?	Would you like to order anything else?

A: DIÁLOGOS

The story: a Spanish married couple who lived and worked for almost 30 years in Germany returns to Spain for their retirement.

Narrator

El señor Manuel Martínez y su esposa Gloria Ruiz llegaron a Alemania hace 29 años para trabajar en una fábrica. Sus tres hijos ya están casados en Alemania y sus nietos son auténticos alemanes. Ni siquiera saben hablar español. Sin embargo, don Manuel y doña Gloria decidieron volver a España. Vendieron su piso en Alemania y compraron una casita en Fuengirola, en la Costa del Sol. Hoy doña Gloria y don Manuel tienen visita. Han invitado a sus nuevos vecinos para conocerlos. Ahora están tomando café y hablando de su vida en Alemania.

Señor Manuel Martínez and his wife Gloria Ruiz went to Germany 29 years ago to work in a factory. Their three children married in Germany and their grandchildren have German citizenship. They don't even speak Spanish. Nevertheless, Doña Gloria and Don Manuel decided to return to Spain. They sold their flat in Germany and bought a small house in Fuengirola on the Costa del Sol. Today, Doña Gloria and Don Manuel have visitors. They have invited their new neighbours around to get to know them. At the moment they are drinking coffee and talking about their life in Germany

Manuel

En Alemania trabajaba en una fábrica de coches, en la Ford, en Colonia, y al principio, Gloria también trabajaba, pero cuando tuvimos los niños, ella dejó de trabajar. Yo ganaba bastante. Trabajaba mucho. Tenía que levantarme a las cinco y media de la mañana y volvía a casa sobre las cuatro de la tarde.

In Germany, I was working in a car factory at Ford's in Cologne and at the beginning Gloria was also working, but when we had the children she stopped working. I was working very hard. I was getting up a half past five in the morning and returning home at around four o'clock in the afternoon.

Guest (Man)

No me digas, a las cinco y media de la mañana te levantabas, ¡qué barbaridad!

You're not telling me you got up at half past five in the morning, how awful!

248

Guest (Woman)
Y dime, vuestros hijos, ¿qué hacen
ahora? ¿Siguen viviendo en Alemania?

Tell me, what are your children
doing now? Are they still in the
Germany?

Gloria
Claro, ya están todos casados y tienen
sus propias familias.

Yes, of course, they are all married
and have their own families.

Guest (Woman)
¿Y no quieren volver a España?

And don't they want to
return to Spain?

Gloria
No, qué va, ¡si casi no saben hablar
español! Ellos están muy bien en
Alemania. Allí tienen su trabajo, su
familia y su casa. No, ellos no quieren
volver a España. ¡Si nacieron todos
en Alemania! Ellos nos visitan en
verano y nosotros los visitamos en
invierno. Está muy bien asi.

No, no, they can hardly speak any
Spanish. They are doing very well
in Germany. They have their work,
their family and their home there.
No, they don't want to return to
Spain. They were all born in
Germany. They visit us in the
summer and we visit them in the
winter. It's very good that way.

Guest (Woman)
Ah, estupendo.

Oh, that's nice.

The story: In the final scene we meet Doña Gloria and Don Manuel again as they
have dinner in the restaurant.

Waiter
Buenas noches, ¿qué van a tomar los
señores? ¿Quieren tomar algún
aperitivo?

Good evening. What are you
(Madam and Sir) going to have?
Would you like an appetizer?

Gloria
Sí, de aperitivo tomaremos unas
tapas de jamón serrano.

Yes, as an appetizer we'll have a
few raw ham hors d'œuvres.

Waiter
¿y para beber?

And to drink?

Manuel
Tomaremos un vino tinto, un Rioja.
Y tráiganos también una botella de
agua mineral sin gas, por favor.

We'll have a red wine, a rioja.
And bring a bottle of still
mineral water as well please.

Waiter
Y de primero, ¿qué van a tomar?

And what will you have for the
first course?

Gloria
Yo una paella valenciana.

I'll have a Valencian paella.

Manuel
Y yo una sopa de pollo.

And I'll have a chicken soup.

Waiter
¿Y de segundo?

And for the main course?

Manuel
De segundo quiero pescado,
tomaré salmón al horno.

For the main course I would like
fish, I'll have fried salmon.

Gloria
Y para mí un solomillo a la plancha.

And for me a grilled fillet steak.

Waiter
Muy bien, ¿quieren pedir algo más?

Good, would you like
anything else?

Manuel
Nada más, muchas gracias.

Nothing else, thank you.

Waiter
Ahora mismo les traigo el aperitivo
y las bebidas.

I'll bring you the appetizer and
drinks immediately.

B: EJERCICIOS

Ejercicio 1:

¿Qué hiciste ayer? Responda que sí – What did you do yesterday?
Reply with yes.

E Ejemplo – Example:

Voz:	*¿Te tomaste una cerveza?*
	Did you drink a beer?
Usted:	*Sí, me tomé una cerveza*
	Yes, I drank a beer.
Voz:	*Sí, me tomé una cerveza.*
Usted:	*Sí, me tomé una cerveza.*

 Y ahora usted, por favor – and now you:

1. ¿Te tomaste una cerveza?
   Sí, me tomé una cerveza.

2. ¿Te comiste una ensalada?
   Sí, me comí una ensalada.

3. ¿Subiste a la primera planta?
   Sí, subí a la primera planta.

4. ¿Jugasteis a las cartas?
   Sí, jugamos a las cartas.

5. ¿Hablasteis sobre vuestra vida
   en Alemania?
   Sí, hablamos sobre nuestra vida
   en Alemania.

Did you drink a beer?
Yes, I drank a beer.

Did you go up to the first floor?
Yes, I went up to the first floor.

Did you go up to the first floor??
Yes, I went up to the first floor.

Did you play cards?
Yes, we played cards.

Did you talk about your life
in Germany?
Yes, we talked about our life
in Germany.

6. ¿Vendisteis el piso en Alemania?
   Sí, vendimos el piso en Alemania.

Did you sell the flat in Germany?
Yes, we sold the flat in Germany.

7. ¿Se quedaron los niños en Alemania?
   Sí, los niños se quedaron
   en Alemania.

Did the children stay in Germany?
Yes, the children stayed in.
Germany

Ejercicio 2:
Utilice el imperfecto – Use the "imperfecto".

CD3
TOP22 **E** **Ejemplo – Example:**

Voz: *Ayer gané mucho dinero.*
           Yesterday I earned a lot of money.

Usted: *Antes también ganaba mucho dinero.*
           Before that I was also earning a lot of money.

Voz: *Antes también ganaba mucho dinero.*

Usted: *Antes también ganaba mucho dinero.*

Y ahora usted, por favor – and now you:

1. Ayer gané mucho dinero.
   Antes también ganaba mucho dinero.

   Yesterday I earned a lot of money.
   Before that I was also earning
   a lot of money.

2. Ayer bebimos mucho vino.
   Antes también bebíamos mucho vino.

   Yesterday we drank too much wine.
   Before that we were also drinking
   too much wine.

3. Ayer Ricardo durmió muchas horas.

   Antes también dormía muchas horas.

   Yesterday Ricardo slept for a long
   time.
   Before that he also sleeping for a
   long time.

4. Ayer Gloria trabajó todo el día.

   Antes también trabajaba todo el día.

   Yesterday Gloria worked for the
   whole day.
   Before that she was also working for
   the whole day.

5. Ayer volví sobre las cuatro de la
   tarde.
   Antes también volvía sobre las
   cuatro de la tarde.

   Yesterday I returned at around four
   o'clock in the afternoon.
   Before that I was also returning at
   around four o'clock in the afternoon.

6. Ayer tuve que levantarme a las seis
   de la mañana.
   Antes también tenía que levantarme
   a las seis de la mañana.

   Yesterday I got up at 6 o'clock.

   Before that I was also getting up
   at 6 o'clock.

7. En verano nos visitaron nuestros
   amigos.
   Antes también nos visitaban nuestros
   amigos.

   In the summer our friends.
   visited us.
   Before that our friends used to
   visit us.

Ejercicio 3:

Dígalo de otra forma – Say it differently.

E **Ejemplo – Example:**

Voz:	*No comas tanto.*
	Don't eat so much.
Usted:	*Deja de comer tanto.*
	Stop eating so much.
Voz:	*Deja de comer tanto.*
Usted:	*Deja de comer tanto.*

 Y ahora usted, por favor – and now you:

1. No comas tanto.   Don't eat so much.
   Deja de comer tanto.   Stop eating so much.

2. No trabajes durante la noche.   Don't work at night.
   Deja de trabajar durante la noche.   Stop working at night.

3. No hables tanto.   Don't speak so much.
   Deja de hablar tanto.   Stop speaking so much.

4. No preguntes.   Don't ask.
   Deja de preguntar.   Stop asking.

5. No bebas tanta cerveza.   Don't drink so much beer.
   Deja de beber tanta cerveza.   Stop drinking so much beer.

6. No juguéis a las cartas.   Don't play cards.
   Dejad de jugar a las cartas.   Stop playing cards.

7. No corras tanto.   Don't walk so quickly.
   Deja de correr tanto.   Stop walking so quicky.

Ejercicio 4:

Dígalo de otra forma – Say it differently.

 Ejemplo – Example:

Voz:	*Me voy a mi casa.*
	I go home.
Usted:	*Me iré a mi casa.*
	I will go home.
Voz:	*Me iré a mi casa.*
Usted:	*Me iré a mi casa.*

 Y ahora usted, por favor – and now you:

1. Me voy a mi casa.
   Me iré a mi casa.

   I go home.
   I will go home.

2. Nos tomamos un café con leche.
   Nos tomaremos un café con leche.

   We drink a white coffee.
   We will drink a white coffee.

3. Puri se casa el domingo que viene.
   Puri se casará el domingo que viene.

   Puri is getting married next Sunday.
   They will rent a flat in San Sebastián.

4. Alquilan un piso en San Sebastián.
   Alquilarán un piso en San Sebastián.

   They rent a flat in San Sebastián.
   They will rent a flat in San Sebastián.

5. Por la tarde dan una vuelta en bicicleta.
   Por la tarde darán una vuelta en bicicleta.

   In the afternoons we go on a bike tour.
   In the afternoons we will go on a bike tour.

6. El fin de semana comemos en un buen restaurante.
El fin de semana comeremos en un buen restaurante.

At the weekend we eat in a good restaurant.
At the weekend we will eat in a good restaurant.

7. De aperitivo tomamos unas tapas de jamón serrano.
De aperitivo tomaremos unas tapas de jamón serrano.

For the appetizer we eat a few raw ham hors d'œuvres.
For the appetizer we will eat a few raw ham hors d'œuvres.

GRAMÁTICA

The "indefinido"

The "indefinido" is the past tense used to describe actions and situations which were completed in the past and happened only once. The use of the "indefinido" in Spanish is not a matter of style but is used to answer the question *What happened*? The imperfect, on the other hand, is used to describe background events which were happening at the time. The imperfect can be used to answer the question "*What was happening*?" or "*What used to happen*?". – i.e. Back then, we were getting up at 6 o'clock in the morning and used to take the bus to work.

The "indefinido" for regular verbs ending in **-ar**, **-er** und **-ir** is formed as follows:

INDEFINIDO

		COMP**RAR**	VEND**ER**	DECID**IR**
	1. Pers.	compré	vendí	decidí
Singular	2. Pers.	compraste	vendiste	decidiste
	3. Pers.	compró	vendió	decidió
	1. Pers.	compramos	vendimos	decidimos
Plural	2. Pers.	comprasteis	vendisteis	desidisteis
	3. Pers.	compraron	vendieron	decidieron

The "indefinido" forms for verbs ending in *-er* and *-ir* are identical. For verbs ending in *-ar* it is only the final vowel which is different. In the first person plural, the "indefinido" forms for verbs ending in *-ar* and *-ir* are the same as the present form.

Example:

*El señor Manuel Martínez y su esposa Gloria Ruiz **llegaron** a Alemania hace 29 años para trabajar en una fábrica. ... **decidieron** volver a España. **Vendieron** su piso en Alemania y compraron una casita en Fuengirola.*	Señor Manuel Martínez and his wife Gloria Ruiz went to Germany 29 years ago to work in a factory (literally: arrived in the Germany) ... they decided to return to Spain. They sold their flat in the Germany and bought a small house in Fuengirola.

Adverbs of Time

Hace is used to refer to a non-specific point in time **before** a period of time being mentioned. Its best translation is "ago".

Examples:

Compramos esta casa hace 18 años.	We bought this house 18 years ago.
Compramos este coche hace 4 años.	We bought this car 4 years ago.

Desde hace is used to refer to a period of time in the past.
Here the best translation is "for".

Examples:

Vivimos en esta casa desde hace 18 años.	We having been living in this house for 18 years.
Tenemos este coche desde hace 4 años.	We've had this car for 4 years.

Desde is used to refer to a non-specific point in time **after** the period of time being mentioned. Its best translation is "since".

Examples:

Vivimos en esta casa desde el año 1981.	We've lived in this house since 1981.
Tenemos este coche desde el año 1995.	We've had this car since 1995.

Supplementary Exercise 1
Use either *hace, desde hace* or *desde*:

Example: Está en mi casa ... ayer. Está en mi casa desde ayer.
1. ... una semana visité a Carmen.
2. No he visto a María ... tres semanas.
3. No ha comido nada ... ayer.
4. No he dormido ... la semana pasada.
5. Encontramos a Luis ... un mes.
6. No he trabajado ... dos semanas.

Other adverbs of time:

ayer	yesterday
antes de ayer	the day before yesterday
mañana	tomorrow
pasado mañana	the day after tomorrow
la semana pasada	last week
la semana que viene	next week
el año pasado	last year
el año que viene	next year

A Summary of the Adverbs of Time

antes de ayer ⇐ ayer ⇐ **hoy** ⇒ mañana ⇒ pasado mañana
el año pasado ⇐ **este año** ⇒ el año que viene
la semana pasada ⇐ esta semana ⇒ la semana que viene

Para – por

Para means "to (or in order to)" or "for":

Trabaja para comer.	He works to eat.
Trabaja para su familia.	He works for his family.

Example:

Llegaron a Alemania para trabajar en una fábrica.	They came to Germany to work in a factory.

The use of the words _para_ and _por_ can cause problems as both words can be translated by "for":

| _Trabaja **para** su familia._ | He works for his family. |
| _Trabaja **por** su familia._ | He works for his family. |

In the first case the family are considered to be the beneficiaries of his work whilst in the second case the family are his reason for his doing the work.

The Diminutive

The use of the diminutive is used a lot more often in Spanish than it is in English and is very widespread in colloquial Spanish. It is formed by adding _-ito/-ita_ to the stem of the noun:

casa	⇒	_cas - ita_
silla	⇒	_sill - ita_
plato	⇒	_plat - ito_
niño	⇒	_niñ - ito_

Example:

Compraron una casita en Fuengirola. They bought a little house in Fuengirola.

In the south the endings _-illo/-illa_ are commonly used, in the north these endings are _-ico/-ica_, and there are others too.

The construction of the diminutive is relatively complicated as there are many exceptions to the above rule.
The following are the most important exceptions:

Words ending in _-n, -r_ or _-e_ having two or more syllables form the diminutive by adding _-cito/-cita, -cillo/-cilla, -cico/-cica:_

mujer	⇒	_mujer - cita_
coche	⇒	_coche - cito_
balcón	⇒	_balcon - cito_

Single syllable words ending in a consonant form the diminutive
by adding *-ecito/ecita:*

sol	⇒	*sol - ecito*
pan	⇒	*pan - ecito* (panecillos are bread rolls)
luz	⇒	*luc - ecita*

What is important to remember is that in Spanish the diminutive is often used
to express emotion. By using the diminutive the speaker is saying that he has a
positive attitude towards the thing he is talking about.

Examples:

¡Qué solecito!	What lovely sunshine!
¿Dónde está mi mujercita?	Where is my dear wife?
¡Por fin, en casita!	Home at last! (in the dear little house)

Supplementary Exercise 2
Form the diminutive for the following nouns.

Example: casa; casita
1. casa
2. coche
3. hombre
4. cama
5. silla
6. calor
7. libro
8. amor

In Spanish, adjectives and other types of word can be used in the diminutive.
This nearly always implies some sort of emotional involvement.

Example:

¡Qué niña más grandecita!	What a big girl!

Sometimes more than one diminutive ending is used in the same word:

Example:
> ¡Ay, mi niña tan chiquititica!

It is best to leave these forms to the locals.

El imperfecto

In the following section Don Manuel talks about everyday life in the UK – here he describes things which occured on repeated occasions in the past:

*En Alemania **trabajaba** en una fábrica de coches, en la Ford, en Colonia, y al principio, Gloria también **trabajaba**, pero cuando llegaron los niños, ella dejó de trabajar. Yo **ganaba** bastante. **Trabajaba** mucho. **Tenía que levantarme** a las cinco y media de la mañana y **volvía** a casa sobre las cuatro de la tarde.*

In Germany, I was working in a car factory at Ford's in Cologne and at the beginning Gloria was also working, but when we had the children she stopped working I was earning enough money. I was working very hard. I was getting up at half past five in the morning and returning home at around four o'clock in the afternoon.

You have already seen that in Spanish, there is a difference in the way that actions are reported which occurred once in the past and actions which continually took place. The latter is conveyed through the "imperfecto".

We discussed the conjugation of the verb *estar* in the "imperfecto" in lesson VII. Let's have a look at how regular verbs are formed in the "imperfecto":

IMPERFECTO

		TRABAJ**AR**	VOLV**ER**	DECID**IR**
	1. Pers.	trabaj**aba**	volv**ía**	decid**ía**
Singular	2. Pers.	trabaj**abas**	volv**ías**	decid**ías**
	3. Pers.	trabaj**aba**	volv**ía**	decid**ía**
	1. Pers.	trabaj**ábamos**	volv**íamos**	decid**íamos**
Plural	2. Pers.	trabaj**abais**	volv**íais**	decid**íais**
	3. Pers.	trabaj**aban**	volv**ían**	decid**ían**

The endings are the same for verbs ending in *-er* and *-ir* , and you will see the repetition of other familiar patterns in the verb endings.

Note: All irregular verbs with the exception of *ser, ir* and *ver*, are regular in the "imperfecto".

Supplementary Exercise 3a
Translate. Remember that habitual actions in the past are conveyed by the "imperfecto".

Example: We were getting up (used to get up) at around 8 o'clock in the morning.
Sobre las ocho de la mañana nos levantábamos.

1. We were getting up at around 8 o'clock in the morning.
2. The train used to arrive at half past six.
3. I was leaving at quarter to eight.
4. I used to stop work at around 4 o'clock.

Supplementary Exercise 3b

Now say the same things using the "indefinido" and remember that using this tense conveys that the action occurred only once.

Example: We got up at around 8 o'clock in the morning. Sobre las ocho de la mañana nos levantamos.

1. We got up at around 8 o'clock in the morning.
2. The train arrived at half past six.
3. I left at a quarter to eight.
4. I stopped work at around 4 o'clock.

Dejar de hacer algo

You have already met the verb *dejar* (to leave). When used with the preposition *de* and a verb in the infinitive, *dejar* mean "to stop or to cease doing something":

dejar de hacer algo	to stop doing something
Gloria dejó de trabajar	Gloria stopped working

Example:

Al principio, Gloria también trabajaba, pero cuando llegaron los niños, ella dejó de trabajar.	At the beginning Gloria was also working, but when we had the children she stopped working.

Bastante

When *bastante* is used on its own or in front of a noun it means "enough" or "quite a lot":

Example:

Gano bastante.	I earn enough or quite a lot.
Gano bastante dinero.	I earn enough money/ quite a lot of money.

When *bastante* is used in conjunction with an adverb its meaning is "quite" (or fairly/pretty):

Example:

La butaca es bastante cómoda.	The armchair is quite comfortable.
Hace bastante frío.	

Hablas bastante rápido.	You speak fairly quickly.

The expression **bastante** comes from the verb **bastar** (to be enough).
   basta – that's enough

Qué va

Qué va is a more emphatic way of saying no which is fairly commonplace.
It conveys the idea of thinking along the wrong lines or barking up the wrong tree.

Examples:

¿Y no quieren volver a España?	And don't they want to return to Spain?
No, qué va, ¡si casi no saben hablar español!	No, not all!!! They hardly speak any Spanish.
¿Sabes hablar chino? – ¡Qué va!	Do you speak Chinese? – No, not a word!!!

The (Emphatic) Particle *si*

The particle *si,* e.g. *¡Si casi no saben hablar español!* is used to add additional emphasis to what is being said. "They don't **even** speak Spanish". It can be used in cases where the speaker wants to indirectly suggest that he is not surprised by something:

Examples:

¡Si es Carmen!	**That's** Carmen!
Si nacieron todos en Alemania.	**All of them** were born in Germany.

Emphatic particles are not used that often in Spanish. It is more common to use gestures, facial expressions or to lower or raise the voice to stress a personal opinion.

The Verb *nacer*

In Spanish the active verb *nacer* corresponds to the English passive form "to be born". In the first person singular of the present tense it has a slight irregularity:

		NACER (Present)
	1. Pers.	*nazco*
Singular	2. Pers.	*naces*
	3. Pers.	*nace*
	1. Pers.	*nacemos*
Plural	2. Pers.	*nacéis*
	3. Pers.	*nacen*

Example:

Nacieron todos en Alemania!	They were all born in Germany.

The verbs **conocer/conducir/traducir** also share the same irregularity:

Te conozco.	I know you.
Conduzco muy bien.	I drive very well.
Traduzco la carta.	I translate the letter.

Supplementary Exercise 4

Use the verb *nacer* in the "indefinido". Say when the persons mentioned were born.

Example: Carlos V (quinto), 1500 ; Carlos quinto nació en mil quinientos.

1. Carlos V, 1500;
2. la reina Isabel, 1451;
3. mi amiga y yo, 1963;
4. tú, 1946.

The Verb *morirse*

The verb **morir** (to die) is usually reflexive in Spanish: *me muero* – I die.
In the present tense of the verb **morir** there is a change in the root vowel:

		MORIR (Present)
	1. Pers.	*muero*
Singular	2. Pers.	*mueres*
	3. Pers.	*muere*
	1. Pers.	*morimos*
Plural	2. Pers.	*morís*
	3. Pers.	*mueren*

Past participle: *muerto*
Continuous form: *muriendo*

The verb **dormir** follows the same pattern.

Examples:

Yo duermo mucho.	I sleep a lot.
He dormido muy bien.	I slept very well.
Sonia está durmiendo.	Sonja is sleeping.

Personal (Direct Object) Pronouns

The personal direct object pronouns differ only slightly from the equivalent indirect object pronouns:

SUMMARY OF PERSONAL PRONOUNS

		SUBJECT	INDIRECT OBJECT		DIRECT OBJECT	
	1. Pers.	yo	**me**	(to me)	**me**	(me)
Singular	2. Pers.	tú	**te**	(to you)	**te**	(you)
	3. Pers.	él	**le**	(to him)	**lo**	(him/it)
		ella	**le**	(to her)	**la**	(her)
		usted (señor)	**le**	(to you)	**lo**	(you)
		usted (señora)	**le**	(to you)	**la**	(you)
	1st Pers.	nosotros	**nos**	(to us)	**nos**	(us)
Plural	2. Pers.	vosotros	**os**	(to you)	**os**	(you)
	3. Pers.	ellos	**les**	(to them)	**los**	(them)
		ellas	**les**	(to them)	**las**	(them)
		ustedes (señores)	**les**	(to you)	**los**	(you)
		ustedes (señoras)	**les**	(to you)	**las**	(you)

Example:

> *Ellos nos visitan en verano y nosotros los visitamos en invierno.*

They visit us in the summer and we visit them in the winter

The use of direct object pronouns varies widely from region to region.

The Future

We have already seen in lesson three that the future can be conveyed, as in English, through the use of the verb *ir* (to go). The first question the waiter asked was:

> *¿Qué **van a tomar** los señores?*   What are you
>   (Sir and Madam) going to have?

To reply Doña Gloria used a different form of the future – the synthetic form, which uses a verb ending instead of an auxiliary verb. This form is not known in English. In Spanish it is used more commonly than than the analytic form (with auxiliary verb):

> *De aperitivo **tomaremos** unas tapas*   For the appetizer we'll have a few
> *de jamón serrano.*   raw ham hors d'œuvres.

In Spanish the most common tense used to express the future is the present tense in conjunction with an expression of time denoting the future. In spoken Spanish this is very common.

Example:
> *Mañana me levanto temprano.*   Tomorrow I'll get up early.
>   (lit: tomorrow I get up early)

The future for regular verbs is formed as follows:

FUTURE

		TOMAR	BEBER	PEDIR
	1. Pers.	tom**aré**	beb**eré**	ped**iré**
Singular	2. Pers.	tom**arás**	beb**erás**	ped**irás**
	3. Pers.	tom**ará**	beb**erá**	ped**irá**
	1. Pers.	tom**aremos**	beb**eremos**	ped**iremos**
Plural	2. Pers.	tom**aréis**	beb**eréis**	ped**iréis**
	3. Pers.	tom**arán**	beb**erán**	ped**irán**

The future forms are regular for all three conjugations. In contrast to other tenses the endings are added to the infinitive rather than to the root of the verb.

In many cases, the future tense can be used in Spanish to imply some sort of assumption.

Example:

Olga estará en Ingleterra "Olga will be in the UK" which really means "I assume that Olga is in the UK.

Supplementary Exercise 5
Express an assumption.

Example: Enrique está trabajando. Estará trabajando.
1. Enrique está trabajando.
2. Los niños están enfermos.
3. Julia no puede venir.
4. Está lloviendo.

The Verb *traer*

The verb *traer* (to bring) is irregular:

		TRAER (Present)
	1. Pers.	traigo
Singular	2. Pers.	traes
	3. Pers.	trae
	1. Pers.	traemos
Plural	2. Pers.	traéis
	3. Pers.	traen
Imperative:	2. Pers. Sing. (tú):	*trae*
forms	3. Pers. Sing. (usted):	*traiga*
	2. Pers. Pl.: (vosotros):	*traed*
	3. Pers. Pl.: (ustedes):	*traigan*

In the imperative the object pronoun is added to the end of the word to form a complete word.

Examples:

¡Tráeme un vaso de agua!	Bring me a glass of water.
¡Traedme la comida!	Bring me the food.
¡Tráiganos pan!	Bring us some bread.
Tráiganos también una botella de agua mineral sin gas, por favor.	Bring us a bottle of still mineral water as well.

The verbs *llevar* and *traer* basically have the same meaning.
Use *traer*, when somebody brings something to you, use *llevar*, when you are asked to take something to somebody.

Example:

Tráeme un café.	Bring me (a cup of) coffee.
Llévale un café a tu padre.	Take (a cup of) coffee to your father.

The Verb *venir* (to come)

		VENIR (Present)
	1. Pers.	*vengo*
Singular	2. Pers.	*vienes*
	3. Pers.	*viene*
	1. Pers.	*venimos*
Plurial	2. Pers.	*venís*
	3. Pers.	*vienen*

We met the imperative forms of *ir* and *venir* in lesson VII.
Their forms in the second person singular can easily be confused.
So try to memorize them:

    ¡ve! OR *¡vete!* –   go!
    ¡ven! –   come!

Information about the Country

El aperitivo

El aperitivo – the appetizer. In Spanish this is not necessarily something which you drink before a meal. In can also be used to mean something that stimulates the appetite such as an hors d'oeuvres which might precede the actual starter or first course.

La tapa

Tapas are small snacks which are served with drinks. In many cities in southern Spain they come free with the drinks. Sometimes a separate charge is made. In southern Spain *tapas* are served automatically and the waiters make sure that the people they are serving don't get the same type of *tapa* twice. This can turn a simple glass of beer or wine into a culinary experience, and if you drink enough, your appetite will be satisfied at the same time. *Tapas* aren't usually served with warm drinks or milk-based drinks.

El jamón

El jamón serrano – raw ham, which is usually hung up to dry in Spain.
El jamón york or *el jamón cocido* – cooked bacon (ham or gammon).

El vino

El vino tinto – red wine; *tinto* is used to mean "red", but only for wine. For other things you can use *rojo* or, in certain cases, *colorado*.
El vino blanco – white wine.
Many restaurants have a *vino de la casa*. This is usually relatively inexpensive.

La Rioja is a region in northern Spain. It is famous for its good wines. *El Rioja* is the wine which comes from *la Rioja*. Another well-known type of wine is *el jerez* (sherry) which comes from Jerez.

Bread and water (el agua y el pan)

In Spain a jug of water (tap water which is usually completely safe to drink) and bread is served with a meal. The water is always free of charge. The bread is sometimes free of charge.
Una jarra de agua – a jug of water.

Primero – segundo – postre

In a restaurant the word *primero* refers to the first course. The complete form is *el primer plato* (literally: the first plate).

Example:
> *Y de primero, ¿qué van a tomar?*

It is normal to have a first course, a main course and a dessert in Spanish restaurants: *el primer plato, el segundo plato* and *el postre*. During the week many restaurants serve a *menú del día* (menu of the day). This always consists of a first and main course, a dessert, bread and sometimes a drink. The *menú del día* is usually a very inexpensive way of eating.

La paella

La paella valenciana: Paella is the national dish of Spain. It consists of rice, vegetables, meat, fish and seafood. Paella was originally a dish which came from Valencia, hence the name *paella valenciana.*

Ways of preparing food

The main ways in which food can be prepared are:

cocido	boiled
frito	fried
al vapor	steamed
a la plancha	grilled; with fat on a griddle
al horno	fried
a la brasa	grilled / barbecued; over an open fire

Examples:

patatas cocidas	boiled potatoes
patatas fritas	fried potatoes/chips/potato crisps
verduras al vapor	steamed vegetables
carne a la plancha	grilled meat
pescado al horno	fried fish
chuleta a la brasa	grilled chop

Solutions to the Supplementary Exercises

Supplementary Exercise 1

1. Hace una semana visité a Carmen.
2. No he visto a María desde hace tres semanas.
3. No ha comido nada desde ayer.
4. No he dormido desde la semana pasada.
5. Encontramos a Luis hace un mes.
6. No he trabajado desde hace dos semanas.

Supplementary Exercise 2

1. casita
2. cochecito
3. hombrecito
4. camita
5. sillita
6. calorcito
7. librito
8. amorcito

Supplementary Exercise 3a

1. Sobre las ocho de la mañana nos levantábamos.
2. A las seis y media en punto llegaba el tren.
3. A las ocho menos cuarto salía.
4. Sobre las cuatro dejábamos de trabajar.

Supplementary Exercise 3b

1. Sobre las ocho de la mañana nos levantamos.
2. A las seis y media en punto llegó el tren.
3. A las ocho menos cuarto salí.
4. Sobre las cuatro dejamos de trabajar.

Supplementary Exercise 4

1. Carlos quinto nació en mil quinientos.
2. La reina Isabel nació en mil cuatrocientos cincuenta y uno.
3. Mi amiga y yo nacimos en mil novecientos sesenta y tres.
4. Tú naciste en mil novecientos cuarenta y seis.

Supplementary Exercise 5

1. Estará trabajando.
2. Estarán enfermos.
3. No podrá venir.
4. Estará lloviendo.

A

a la plancha	fried in own fat; grilled
a mano derecha	on the right hand side
a mano izquierda	on the left hand side
abril, el	April
abuela, la	grandmother
abuelo, el	grandfather
abuelos, los	grandparents
aceite, el	oil
adelantar	to overtake
adelante	come in; off you go!
además	besides
adiós	good bye
afeitarse	to shave
agente comercial, el	travelling salesman
agente de aduanas, el	customs officer
agente de policía, el	policeman
agente inmobiliario, el	estate agent
agente secreto, el	secret agent
agente, el	agent; representative; conveyor; civil servant; employee
agosto, el	August
agradable	pleasant
agua mineral, el	mineral water
agua, el (fem.)	water
ahora	now
aire acondicionado, el	air conditioning
ajedrez, el	chess
al final	at the end
al horno	baked
al lado de	next to
al principio	at the beginning
al vapor	steamed
alegrarse	to be happy/glad
alegre	happy; glad
Alemania	Germany
alemán	German
algo	something
algodón, el	cotton
algún, -a	some; many

Alhambra, la	Moorish palace in Granada
allí	there; (over) there
almorzar	to eat lunch
almuerzo, el	lunch
alpinismo, el	mountain climbing
alquilar	to rent; (to sb. or from sb.)
alto, -a	high
altura, la	height
ama de casa, la/el	housewife
amarillo	yellow
amigo, el	friend
amor mío	darling (lit: my love)
anda	come on; off you go!
animal, el	animal
año nuevo, el	New Year
año, el	year
anterior	previous
antes	earlier
antes de ayer	the day before yesterday
antiguo, -a	old
aparcar	to park
aparte	additionally
aperitivo, el	aperitif
aprender	to learn
aquel, -la	those there
aquí	here
Argentina	Argentina
armario, el	cupboard
arquitecto, el/la	architect (male/female)
arreglarse	to get ready
asunto, el	affair; business
auténtico, -a	real; authentic
autobús, el	bus
autopista, la	motorway
autovía, la	road ('A' road or main road)
avión, el	aeroplane
ayer	yesterday
ayudar	to help

azúcar, el	the sugar
azul	blue

B   CD4 TOP 2

bachillerato, el	sixth-form (college)
badminton, el	badminton
bailar	to dance
bajo, -a	low
balcón, el	balcony
balón, el	ball
baloncesto, el	basketball
balonmano, el	handball
bañador, el	swimming costume; swimming trunks
banco, el	bank
bañera, la	bathtub
baño, el	bath
barato, -a	cheap
barriga, la	belly
bastante	enough; quite a lot
bastar	to suffice; to be enough
bebé, el	baby
beber	to drink
bebida, la	drink
biblioteca, la	library
bicicleta, la	bicycle
bien (Adv.)	good
bienvenido, -da	welcome
billete, el	banknote
blanco, -a	white
bocadillo, el	sandwich; open sandwich
bolsa, la	bag
bonito, -a	beautiful
botella, la	bottle
brazo, el	arm
buenas noches	good evening; good night
buenas tardes	good day
bueno (Particle)	so
bueno, -a	good; nice

buenos días	good morning; good day
burro, el	donkey
buscar	to look for
butaca, la	armchair

C   CD4 TOP 3

caballero, el	gentleman (cavalier)
caballo, el	horse
cabeza, la	head
cabra, la	goat
café con leche, el	coffee (white)
café solo, el	coffee (black)
café solo, el	coffee (black)
café, el	coffee
cafetería, la	café
caja fuerte, la	safe
caja, la	box; carton
cajero automático, el	cash dispenser
calcetín, el	sock
calefacción central, la	central heating
caliente	hot
calle, la	street/road (within a town or village)
calor, el	heat; warmth
cama de matrimonio, la	marital bed
cama individual, la	single bed
cama, la	bed
camarero, el	waiter
cambiar	to change; to exchange
caminar	to go walking
camino, el	path
camión, el	lorry
camisa, la	shirt
campo, el	country
campo, el	area
cansado, -a	tired; exhausted
cantar	to sing
cántaro, el	pot
cantidad, la	amount; quantity
cargar	to load

cariño	treasure (term of endearment)
carne de lidia, la	meat from the bull fight
carne, la	meat
carnet de conducir, el	driving license
carnet de identidad, el	identity card
caro, -a	expensive
carretera, la	country road (minor road)
carta, la	letter
cartas, las	game of cards
casa, la	house
casado, -a	married
casarse	to get married; to marry
casi	almost
castellano, el	Spanish (the standard Spanish language)
Castilla	Castilian
catalán, el	Catalonian
Cataluña	Catalonia
ceda el paso	give way
cena, la	evening meal (dinner)
cenar	to eat dinner
céntrico, -a	central
centro, el	(city) centre
cerca	near; nearby
cerdo, el	pig
cerveza, la	beer
ciclismo, el	cycling
cierto, -a	true
cinturón de seguridad, el	seatbelt
circulación, la	traffic; circulation
ciudad, la	city/town
claro, -a	bright; clear
clase, la	class
clima, el	climate
cocer	to boil
coche, el	car
cocina, la	kitchen
colegio, el	primary school
Colonia	Cologne
color, el	colour
colorado, -a	red
comedor, el	dining room
comer	to eat
comida, la	meal
como	like
¿cómo?	how?
cómodo, -a	comfortable
compañero, el	pal; colleague
comprar	to buy
con	with
conducir	to drive
conductor, el	driver
conocer	to get to know
consulado, el	consulate
continuar	to continue
controlar	to check; to control
copa, la	glass (with stem)
correcto	correct; that's right
correr	to run
cortar	to cut
cosmética, la	cosmetics
costa, la	coast
costar	to cost
costumbre, la	custom; habit
creer	to believe
cruce, el	crossroads
¿cuál?	which?
cuando	when
¿cuánto?	how much?
cuarto de baño, el	bathroom
cuarto de estar, el	living room
cubiertos, los	cutlery
cucaracha, la	cockroach
cuchara, la	spoon
cuchillo, el	knife
cuello, el	neck
cuenta corriente, la	current account
cuenta, la	account; bill
cuero, el	leather
cultura, la	culture
curso de español, el	Spanish language course

chaqueta, la	jacket
cheque, el	cheque
chicos, los	children (lit: the little ones)
chino, -a	Chinese
chocolate, el	chocolate
churros, los (Pl.)	pastries

D

CD4 TOP 4

D.N.I. (Documento Nacional de Identidad)	identity card
dar	to give
de	from; of
de acuerdo	agreed
de colores	colourful
de día	during the day
de nada	don't mention it
de noche	at night
de turismo	on tour
debajo de	under
decidir	to decide
decir	to say
dejar	to leave
dejar de hacer algo	to stop doing something
delante de	in front of
demasiado, -a	too + adjective; too much
dentista, el	dentist
dentro de	inside
deporte, el	sport
desayunar	to have breakfast
desayuno, el	breakfast
descargar	to unload
desde hace	for
desear	to wish
despensa, la	larder
despertar	to wake
despertarse	to wake up
después	later; afterwards
desvío provisional, el	(temporary) diversion
detrás de	behind

día, el	day
diciembre, el	December
diente, el	tooth
dinero, el	money
director, el	conductor; director
dirigir	to conduct; to direct
disco, el	record; disc
discoteca, la	discothèque
discutir	to discuss; also: to argue
doblar	to fold; to bend
documentación, la	papers; documents
dólar, el	dollar
doler	to hurt
dolor, el	pain
domingo, el	Sunday
dominó, el	game of dominoes
¿dónde?	where?
dormir	to sleep
dormitorio, el	bedroom
ducha, la	shower
ducharse	to shower
durante	during
duro, el	5-peseta coin

E

CD4 TOP 5

económico, -a	reasonable (of price)
educación infantil, la	infant school
educación primaria, la	primary school
educación secundaria, la	secondary school
elector, el	voter
electrónica, la	electronics
elegante	elegant
elegir	to choose; to elect
ella	her, she (singular)
ellas	them, they (feminine, plural)
ellos	them, they (masculine plural)
él	he
embarazada	pregnant
en casa	at home
en efectivo	in cash

en punto	exactly	*éstos*	these
encantado, -a	pleased	*estrella, la*	star
	(to meet you)	*estudiante, el/la*	student; pupil
encantador, -a	charming	*estudiar*	to learn; to study; to
encantar	to like a lot; lit:		go to school
	to enchant	*excelente*	excellent
encima de	on; over		
encontrar	to find; to meet		
encontrarse	to be situated		

F

enero, el	January	*fábrica, la*	factory
enfermo, -a	ill	*familia, la*	family
ensalada, la	salad	*famoso, -a*	famous
enseñar	to show	*farmacia, la*	pharmacy
entender	to understand	*febrero, el*	February
entonces	then	*fiebre, la*	fever
entrada, la	admission;	*fiesta, la*	party; celebration
	admission ticket	*firmar*	to sign
entrada, la	entrance	*flamenco, el*	flamenco
entre	between; among	*flor, la*	flower
equipar	to equip; to fit out	*formación profesional, la*	technical college
escalar montañas	to climb mountains	*Francia*	France
escribir	to write	*fregadero, el*	sink
escritor, el	writer	*freír*	to fry
escuela, la	school	*fresa, la*	strawberry
ese, -a	that	*frigorífico, el*	refrigerator
espalda, la	back	*frío, -a*	cold
España	Spain	*frío, el*	cold
especial	special; particular	*fruta, la*	fruit
espejo, el	mirror	*fuerte*	strong
espléndido, -a	splendid; wonderful	*funcionar*	to function
esposa, la	wife (spouse)	*fútbol, el*	football
esposo, el	husband (spouse)		
esposos, los	married couple		

G

esquiar	to ski	*Galicia*	Galicia
estación del año, la	season	*gallego, el*	Galician
estación, la	station	*galleta, la*	biscuit
estanco, el	state-run shop	*ganar*	to earn; to win
	selling tobacco pro-	*garganta, la*	throat
	ducts and stamps	*gas, el*	(carbon dioxide);
estantería, la	shelf		gas
estar	to be; to exist; to be	*gato, el*	cat
	situated	*gente, la*	people
este, -a	this here	*ginecólogo, el*	gynaecologist
este, el	east; the East		

Giralda, la	monumental tower in Seville; symbol of Seville
golf, el	golf
gracias	thank you
granada, la	pomegranate; grenade
granadino, -a	Grenadine
grande	large
gris	grey
grúa, la	tow-truck; crane
guardería, la	nursery school (building)
guía de hoteles, la	hotel guide
guía gastronómica, la	restaurant (lit: gastronomic) guide
guía telefónica, la	telephone book or list
guía turística, la	tourist guide (female)
guía turístico, el	tourist guide (male)
guía, la	guide (person – female); the guide (book)
gustar	to like

H CD4 TOP 8

habitación doble, la	double room
habitación individual, la	single room
habitación sencilla, la	single room
habitación, la	room
hablar	to speak
hace	ago; for
hacer	to do
hambre, el	the hunger
hasta	until
hasta la próxima vez	until the next time
hasta la vista	good bye
hasta luego	cheerio (see you later)
hasta pronto	see you soon
hay	there is / there are
hermana, la	sister

hermano, el	brother
hija, la	daughter
hijo, el	son
hola	hello
hombre, el	man; human being
hora de irse	time to go
hora, la	hour
hormiga, la	ant
hornilla de gas, la	gas cooker
horno, el	oven
hospital, el	hospital
hostal, el	hostel
hotel, el	hotel
hoy	today
huelga, la	strike
huelguista, el/la	striker (person on strike)

I CD4 TOP 9

idea, la	idea
idioma, el	language
impreso, el	form
incluido, -a	included
informática, la	IT (information technology)
inglés, el	English
inodoro, el	toilet
instituto (de bachillerato), el	sixth-form (college)
inteligente	intelligent
interesante	interesting
interruptor, el	switch
invierno, el	winter
invitar	to invite
ir	to go
ir en bicicleta	to ride a bicycle
irse	to leave
isla, la	island
italiano, -a	Italian

J

CD4 TOP10

jabón, el	soap
jamón cocido, el	cooked ham
jamón serrano, el	raw ham
jamón york, el	cooked ham
jamón, el	the ham
jarra, la	jug
jerez, el	sherry
jersey, el	pullover; jersey
jueves, el	Thursday
jugar	to play
julio, el	July
junio, el	June
juntos, -as	together

K

CD4 TOP11

kilo, el	kilo

L

CD4 TOP12

lana, la	wool
lavabo, el	wash basin
lavadora, la	washing machine
lavavajillas, el	dishwasher
leche, la	milk
lechuga, la	lettuce
leer	to read
lejos	far away
levantarse	to get up
libre	free
librería, la	book department; book shop
libro, el	book
límite de tiempo, el	time limit
límite de velocidad, el	speed limit
limón, el	lemon
llamarse	to call oneself; to be called
llave, la	key
llegar	to arrive
llevar	to bring; to fetch
llover	to rain

lotería de navidad, la	Christmas lottery
lucir	to shine
luego	later; afterwards
lunes, el	Monday
luz, la	light

M

CD4 TOP13

madre, la	mother
madrileño, -a	(person) from Madrid;
mal (Adv.)	bad
malo, -a	bad; ill
mamá	Mummy
mañana	tomorrow
mañana, la	morning
mandarina, la	mandarin
mano, la	hand
mantequilla, la	butter
manzana, la	apple
mapa, el	map (street map)
maquillarse	to put on makeup
máquina, la	machine
maquinista, el/la	machinist
maravilloso, -a	wonderful; marvellous
marcharse	to leave; to walk away
marco, el	Mark (DM)
marido, el	husband
marisco, el	seafood
marrón	brown
martes, el	Tuesday
marzo, el	March
más	more
mayo, el	May
mecánico, el	mechanic
médico, el	doctor
mediodía, el	midday
mejor	better
menú del día, el	menu of the day
merendar	to drink coffee

merienda, la	light snack in the late afternoon where coffee is drunk
mermelada, la	jam; marmalade
mes, el	month
mesa, la	table
mesita de noche, la	bedside table
metro, el	meter; tube (underground railway)
mi	my (poss. pronoun)
miércoles, el	Wednesday
minibar, el	mini bar
mío	mine (pronoun on its own)
misma, la	the same
mismo, el	the same
moda, la	fashion
momento, el	moment
montaña, la	mountain
morir(se)	to die
mosquito, el	mosquito
motocicleta, la (moto, la)	motorcycle; moped
muchas gracias	many thanks
mucho (Adv.)	very
mucho gusto	It's a pleasure (to meet you)
mucho, -a (Adj.)	a lot; much
muela, la	molar
mujer, la	wife
multa, la	fine
mundo, el	world
museo, el	museum
muy	very

N CD4 TOP14

nada	nothing
nadar	to swim
naranja, la	orange
natación, la	swimming
naturaleza, la	nature
naturalmente	naturally
navidad, la	Christmas
negro	black

nevar	to snow
ni ... ni	neither ... nor
ni siquiera	not once
nieta, la	granddaughter
nieto, el	grandson
nietos, los	grandchildren
niña, la	child (fem.), the girl
niño, el	child (masc.), the boy
nivel de alcohol permitido, el	alcohol limit
nivel de ruido permitido, el	noise threshold
nivel permitido, el	limit (lit: the permitted level)
no	no; not
no importa	it doesn't matter
noche, la	night
nombre, el	name
norte, el	north; the North
nosotros	we
noviembre, el	November
novio/a, el/la	boyfriend/bridegroom; girlfriend/bride
nublado	cloudy
nuestro	our
nuevo, -a	new
número, el	number
nunca	never

O CD4 TOP15

obligatorio, -a	compulsory
obligatorio, -a (Adj.)	compulsory
obra, la	building site
octubre, el	October
oeste, el	west; the West
oferta, la	special offer
oficina central, la	head office
oficina de correos, la	post office
oficina de empleo, la	job centre; employment office
oficina de turismo, la	tourist office

oficina, la	office; bureau; workshop; chambers (lawyer); public office
oído, el	ear; hearing
oír	to hear; to listen
olla, la	pot
oreja, la	ear; outer ear
oscuro, -a	dark
otoño, el	autumn
otro, -a	other; another

P
CD4
TOP 16

padre, el	father
paella, la	paella (Spanish national dish)
pagar	to pay
País Vasco, el	the Basque country
país, el	country; land
pan, el	bread
pantalones, los	trousers
papel, el	paper
papelería, la	stationery department; stationer's shop
papeles, los	papers
paquete, el	parcel; package
para	for; in order to
parecer	to appear; to seem
parte, la	part; piece
pasado mañana	the day after tomorrow
pasado, -a	last; past
pasaporte, el	passport
pasar	to pass; to spend
pasillo, el	corridor; passage; hallway
paso, el	passageway; gateway
patata, la	potato
patatas fritas, las	chips; crisps
pediatra, el	pediatrician
pedir	to order; to request

pelar	to peel
pelota, la	ball
peluca, la	wig
peluquería, la	hairdresser's salon
Península Ibérica, la	the Iberian peninsula
pensar	to think; to believe
pensión, la	guest house
peor	worse
pequeño, -a	small
pera, la	pear
perdonar	to excuse; to forgive; to pardon
perdón	pardon; forgiveness
perfume, el	perfume
perfumería, la	perfumery
permitir	to allow; to permit
pero	but
perro, el	dog
pescadería, la	fishmonger's shop
pescado, el	fish
peseta, la	peseta
pianista, el/la	pianist (masc./fem.)
piano, el	piano
pié, el	foot
piel, la	skin; leather
pierna, la	leg
pieza, la	piece
pimienta, la	pepper
pimiento, el	pepper (vegetable)
Pirineos, los	the Pyrenees
piso, el	floor; flat
pizza, la	pizza
plan, el	map; plan
planta baja, la	ground floor
planta sótano, la	basement
planta, la	floor
plátano, el	banana
plato, el	plate
playa, la	beach
plaza, la	square
(un) poco	a little
poder	to be able to

policía, el/la	policeman/police-woman
política, la	politics
pollo, el	chicken
poner	to lay; to place; to give; to serve
por	for
por aquí	here in the vicinity
por ejemplo	for example
por favor	please
por supuesto	of course
¿por que?	why?
porque	because
posibilidad, la	possibility, opportunity
posible	possible
postre, el	dessert
precio, el	price
preferir	to prefer
pregunta, la	question
preguntar	to ask
preparar	to prepare
primavera, la	spring
príncipe, el	prince
probador, el	changing cubicle
probar	to try
probarse	to try on
problema, el	problem
producir	to manufacture; to produce
productor, el	manufacturer; producer
prohibir	to forbid; to prohibit
protesta, la	protest; objection
provincia, la	district; county
puerta, la	door
pues	so

Q   CD4 TOP17

¿qué?	what?
quedarse	to remain; to stay
querer	to want

queso, el	cheese
¿quién?	who?

R   CD4 TOP18

rápido, -a	fast; quick
recibidor, el	hallway
recoger	to collect
recto	straight ahead
regular	to control; to regulate
reina, la	queen
relación, la	relation
rellenar	to complete; to fill in
reservar	to reserve
resguardo, el	receipt
restaurante, el	restaurant
retirar	to remove; to withdraw
reunión de negocios, la	business meeting
reunión política, la	political gathering
reunión, la	meeting; gathering
reunirse	to meet; to gather
rey, el	king
rioja, el	wine from the la Rioja region
Rioja, la	a region of Spain
rojo, -a	red
sábado, el	Saturday

S   CD4 TOP19

saber	to know; to be able to
sacar	to fetch; to withdraw (money)
sacarina, la	saccharine; sweeteners
sal, la	salt
salida, la	exit
salir	to go out; to set off; to leave

salita, la	living room (family room)	*suelo, el*	ground
salmón, el	salmon	*sueño, el*	tiredness
salón, el	lounge (more formal)	*supermercado, el*	supermarket
		sur, el	south; the South
sartén, la	frying pan		
sección, la	department		**CD4** TOP20
secretaria, la	secretary	**_T_**	
sed, la	thirst	*tableta de chocolate, la*	bar of chocolate
seguir	to continue	*talla, la*	size (around waist)
sello, el	postage stamp; stamp	*también*	also; too
semáforo, el	traffic lights	*tanto (Adv.)*	so very much; so long; so many
semana, la	week	*tanto, -a (Adj)*	so much; so large; so long; such
señor, el	gentleman	*tapa, la*	small snack; canapé
señora, la	lady; wife	*tarde*	late
sentarse	to sit down	*tarde, la*	afternoon
septiembre, el	September	*tarjeta de crédito, la*	credit card
ser	to be	*taxi, el*	taxi
servicio, el	toilet	*taza, la*	cup
siempre	always	*té, el*	tea
siesta, la	afternoon nap; siesta	*teléfono, el*	telephone
		televisión, la	television
siguiente, el	next	*temprano, -a*	early
silla, la	chair	*tenedor, el*	fork
simpático, -a	sympathetic; nice	*tener*	to have
sin	without	*tenis de mesa, el*	table tennis
sin embargo	anyhow; anyway; however	*tenis, el*	tennis
		terraza, la	terrace; large balcony; roof terrace
sintético, -a	synthetic		
sitio, el	place		
sí	yes	*terremoto, el*	earthquake
sobre	over; above	*tiempo, el*	time
sobre (+ time phrase)	around	*típico, -a*	typical
sobrepasar	to exceed	*tocólogo, el*	midwife
sofá, el	sofa	*todavía*	still; yet
sol, el	sun	*todo*	entire; whole
solo	only; alone	*todo el mundo*	everyone
solomillo, el	sirloin	*tomar*	to consume; to eat; to drink; to take
soltero, -a	single; unmarried		
sopa, la	soup	*tomate, el*	tomato
sótano, el	cellar	*tonto, -a*	silly
su	his/her	*tormenta, la*	storm
subir	to go up; to ascend	*toro, el*	bull

toros, los	bullfight (lit: the bulls)
tostada, la	toast; toasted bread
trabajar	to work
trabajo, el	work
traducir	to translate
traductor, el	translator
traer	to bring; to fetch
tráfico, el	traffic
tren, el	train
tropical	tropical
tu	your
turista, el	tourist
turno, el	shift; turn
tú	you

U
CD4 TOP21

un; una	a; an
universidad, la	university
usted (Sing.), ustedes (Pl.)	you (polite from)
uva, la	grape

V
CD4 TOP22

vaca, la	cow
vacaciones, las	vacation; holiday
vale	OK
valenciano, -a	Valencian; from Valencia
vapor, el	steam
vaqueros, los	jeans
varios	several; some; various
vasco, -a	Basque
vaso, el	glass
vecino, el	neighbour
vehículo, el	vehicle
vender	to sell
venir	to come
ventana, la	window
ver	to see

verano, el	summer
verdad, la	truth
verde	green
verdura, la	vegetable
vestido, el	dress
vestirse	to get dressed
veterinario, el	veterinary surgeon
viajar	to travel
viaje, el	journey; trip
vida, la	life
viento, el	wind
viernes, el	Friday
vino tinto, el	red wine
vino, el	wine
visita guiada, la	guided tour
visita, la	visit
visitar	to visit
vivir	to be alive; to live
volcán, el	volcano
volver	to go back; to return
vosotros	you
vuestro, -a	your

W
CD4 TOP23

wáter, el	loo

Y
CD4 TOP24

ya	already
ya no	no longer
yo	I
yogur, el	yoghurt

Z
CD4 TOP25

zanahoria, la	carrot
zapatos, los	shoes
zona, la	zone
zumo, el	juice